To Frances. Stanley
with all best wishes

Henra Ayer

D1609891

AN AMBASSADOR SPEAKS OUT

AN AMBASSADOR SPEAKS OUT

Speeches and Writings

by

Shlomo Argov

THE VAN LEER JERUSALEM FOUNDATION

JERUSALEM

WEIDENFELD AND NICOLSON

LONDON

First published in Great Britain by
George Weidenfeld & Nicolson Limited
91 Clapham High Street, London SW4 7TA
1983

ISBN 0 297 78260 6

Typesetting by "Daf-Chen", Ltd., Jerusalem, Israel
Printed and bound in Great Britain

Contents

Preface

It is indeed a timely idea to publish a selection of the speeches, articles and letters of Shlomo Argov.

Because of the tragic circumstances that ended his mission in London, he has become a symbol of the Israeli diplomat who today not only fights for his country's cause under most difficult circumstances, but also risks his very life in doing so.

Shlomo Argov has deep roots in Israel and in everything it represents. He is the descendant of a family which has lived in Jerusalem for seven generations. One of his ancestors became the founder of Petach Tikvah, the first Jewish village, founded in the 19th century. Since his teens when, as a member of the Palmach he was wounded in the 1948 War of Independence, his life has been dedicated to the service of his people.

I have known Shlomo Argov since his days as a student in Washington, D.C., when he also did part-time work at the Israel Embassy to earn his living. At a later stage I managed to convince him to work with me in the Prime Minister's Office, under David Ben-Gurion. There he was connected with the Point-Four Programmes and with manpower policies, and he became an active part of the nerve centre of the Ministry.

When the late Ehud Avriel asked him to join the Foreign Office at our first Embassy in Ghana, I tried my best to dissuade him and urged him to devote his talents to the home front, which I regarded as more important than any service abroad.

His entire career, as illustrated in this book, proves that in this particular case I most certainly was wrong. Shlomo applied himself to the Foreign Service with a particular single-mindedness, regarding it as both a profession and a mission in life. He aspired to perfection and never relented in his efforts in search of new ways to fight more effectively on the diplomatic front for the just cause of Israel.

The book's contents not only provide a profound analysis of the issues at stake for Israel, they also demonstrate the eloquent and persuasive words that Shlomo Argov has always found to present his country's message.

Jerusalem, November 1982   TEDDY KOLLEK

1
Israel

The "Many Israels"

Address to the Joint Israel Appeal
Rabbinical and Communal Leaders
on the eve of Yom Kippur
London, September 16, 1981

I would like to talk to you tonight, if I may, about the Israel that we were once supposed to have loved; the Israel which some say, used to exist but is no longer; the Israel that until not so long ago was the subject of our abiding love and admiration and which today is allegedly less so. Such are some of the things that are being said today about Israel.

Now which Israel are these critics — the mournful and the gleeful — referring to? Is there really one particular Israel? Or are there perhaps many Israels? How for example does one explain our having had to contend of late and at one and the same time with complaints by very orthodox Jews about some terrible things which we are supposed to be doing in Jerusalem and by those of other no less concerned and devoted Jews about other allegedly equally terrible things which very orthodox Jews are themselves doing in that same Jerusalem? How does one account for, let alone reconcile, the clash between those people who, while claiming to be Jews, were nonetheless capable of demonstrating outside the Embassy of Israel in London waving signs saying "Death to Zionism" and "Begin is a Nazi criminal", and the angry protestations of

3

other Jews deeply concerned about what they perceive to be an encroachment on academic freedom and a threat to scientific research — this time to the unearthing of the glories of our past?*

To each apparently his own Jerusalem. To each his own complaints, and these are almost infinite. Some complain about the noise, others about the oppressive stillness of the Sabbath, some about the conduct of individuals in public, others about the quality of public life. All join in the same refrain: things are not what they used to be. Nothing is what it used to be. But what was this "it" that used to be? Was there in fact any one single identifiable "it"? Was there ever one precise Israel, one single variation of "Jerusalem"? Or were there perhaps always "many Israels" and "many Jerusalems"? Was Israel not, and will it not always be a composite, a tapestry of all the myriad strains and strands of the Jewish people? And was not, and will not Israel always remain a repository of all the colours and the shades *and* the shadows of the Jewish experience across the millennia? Israel never was, neither will it, nor should it ever be the exclusive expression of any one facet of Jewishness; nor must it ever become the exclusive preserve of any one community, nor be expected to model itself in its image.

Jewish variety, diversity and complexity — that is the hallmark of Israel. That is what Israel is all about. Not the preserve of anyone but the refuge of *everyone* along with their entire bag and baggage, the good *and* the bad. We never said "No" to anyone. All were welcome. *Beruhim*

---

* Editor's note: this remark is referring to the City of David excavations near the Temple Mount in Jerusalem.

Haba'im is the greeting accorded to all. Blessed are those who come, from wherever they come. And they have in fact come from everywhere.

There were once upon a time the Eastern European Jews — those who more than anyone laid the physical foundations for the State of Israel. Those who grasped and seized the land literally with their bare hands and led the return to the *soil* of Israel as much as to the *land* of Israel — until catastrophe struck and they and the rest of the Jews of Europe were no more. Just when the structure of Zion Rebuilt was ready to receive their teeming millions.

But these were not the only Jews who returned to the land. Over centuries others made their way back from all the exiles of the East. And they too came in the name of Zion. They came quietly and settled quietly. Their concept of Zionism was not the tilling of soil, the sowing of seeds and the harvesting of the crops. These Jews hugged the walls, sat by the stones and prayed at the tombs of their ancestors. That was their form of Zionism and it was just as effective.

And then there were those Jews who always dwelt within the walls of the ancient capital and took up the cause of Zionism before that term was ever conceived. Before the ordeal of Captain Dreyfus and the clarion call of Theodor Herzl. Their concept and practice of Zionism was to break out of the walls of old Jerusalem. To brave the dangers of their times and to lay the foundations for the Jerusalem of our times — Nahlat Shiva and Yemin Moshe — names no less illustrious than any in the entire land. They called them "quarters" then. Today they would be known as "settlements". Thus they all came together — the original components of the mosaic that is Israel today.

5

The first ingathering of the exiles that was to be joined by the multitudes that were to come in later years and to form the "many Israels" of today.

There are many other Israels — other contradictions, other paradoxes. There is a mighty Israel. There is a fighting Israel. There is an Israel which can within a matter of minutes knock out an atomic reactor and return unscathed. There has been throughout these thirty-three years of its independence a powerful, mighty, invincible Israel, which has protected itself against immense odds and triumphed every time it was put to the test. A mighty, powerful Israel. An Israel of sophistication, of advanced technology, of inventiveness and improvisation, of daring and innovation. In this very Michael House where we meet today are to be seen some of the products of the remarkable industry that we have created in Israel. Marks and Spencer would not buy them were they not of the highest quality. And these are but some of the fruits of the tremendous industrial and technological revolution which has taken place in Israel following upon one of the world's greatest agricultural revolutions whose products too we see at Marks and Spencer stores and elsewhere. They would not be sold by them unless they conformed to — or better still — surpassed the highest standards.

And yet there is another Israel. There is the Israel of the underprivileged. The Israel of the uneducated. The Israel of those who have yet to be brought into the mainstream of the society, who live on the fringes of affluence and therefore the fringes also of national life and who are resentful because of the non-fulfillment of their dreams. That too is a very important and integral part of Israel.

There are many Israels. Like the colours of the rainbow.

So we were meant to be. Not a monolithic entity, not a dull unitary block but an exciting assortment of everything that the Jewish world is capable of producing, plus all of the warts and the wrinkles of two thousand years of the most tragic turbulence that any nation could possibly experience — dispersion, persecution, physical assault and battery and the constant psychological war that was waged against us. We have been in confrontation with the rest of the world since the very day we came into being and nowhere and at no time was this confrontation more intense, more abrasive and more painful than when we lived among the rest of the world. The world was unkind to us for almost as many centuries as we have lived in it.

There are "many Israels" but there is one thing that is constant. All these "many Israels" are still threatened, are still the subject and the target of a massive effort — as massive an effort as has ever been waged — against the very foundations, the very raison d'être, of the State of Israel. Not this or that policy, not this or that act or action but the very idea of a Jewish State is once again being questioned if not contested.

I have dwelt on this dimension not in order to divert attention or to distract from our other ills and woes, including some allegedly of our own making. I am not pointing at the enemy without in order to cover up the deficiencies within. I am pointing to the enemy outside because repelling it is still our number-one priority.

The task of securing the state and the people of Israel has yet to be completed. May we only be spared more bloodshed. But the securing of Israel is not only a function of arms and armaments, of strategies and tactics, of implements of war and of techniques of war. There is no way in which the physical securing of Israel can ever be fully accomplished unless we achieve the social, the national — the *internal* — securing of the people of Israel.

There have recently been disturbing instances of friction; of abrasive dialogue and shrill polemics; of divisions and disagreements. Most disturbing have been those recent manifestations of inter-community tensions of the kind that we thought were easing up and that with time would dissolve altogether. But then there has not been that much time. It has after all only been thirty-three years since we became masters of our own destiny. The friction of diverse backgrounds and of different cultural experiences are apparently still with us. Jews did not all live in one shtetl or one mellah (North African ghetto). Some lived in shtetls and others lived in mellahs and all were respectively conditioned by their different immediate environments. These have all come together now in the State of Israel and form its "many Israels". And there is not only friction but also resentment. Some have fared better because they brought with them from their countries of origin some of that wherewithal which enables one to progress more easily than another. Others were not so privileged. It is to this disparity that we now need to address ourselves. And we need to do this urgently and effectively. Not in panic, nor in haste, but sensibly and courageously. The effort called for involves a massive investment and this is precisely the area in which a joint Israel-Diaspora enterprise needs to be launched. This is the one area which is yours for the asking. The rest is our responsibility and burden. If need be, we will do this by ourselves too, but then you will have missed out on meeting together with us one of the great Jewish challenges of our time.

8

There has to be now an investment in *human* infrastructure. We have invested in a military infrastructure. We have invested in an economic infrastructure. We have invested in a marvellous educational infrastructure. We have invested in a scientific infrastructure. We now need to invest — not for the first time but with particular emphasis — in people. In those very people who make up the "many Israels" that are Israel. Not in order that these "many Israels" should melt and disappear in a new monolithic entity, but rather that they should rise and attain those levels and standards which have been set by those more privileged than themselves in order to form together one harmonious, variegated and colourful Israel.

Ours are legitimate problems. They are understandable problems. They are inevitable problems. They are the consequences of an *experience*. The consequence of a saga, an odyssey, across all of the dispersals and the dispersions of this world. That is what they are. And they have all gathered together in Israel as all of our ingathering exiles brought with them bagfuls of all that had been accumulated in the course of our long historical march.

Fear not, Israel is a vital, viable, vibrant and beautiful country. It *has* blemishes, but then who hasn't? Let us join hands in order to put right what still needs to be put right so that we can be ever more proud of our State of Israel. So that no one will ever say to you that the Israel you loved is no longer there. The Israel that you loved *is* there and will *always* be there and is deserving of all your love. Shana Tova!

Some Reflections on
Israel's Thirtieth Anniversary

The Netherlands, April 1978

Reflecting recently on the mood in Israel today, an experienced observer of the Israeli scene bemoaned the resurgence in the country of what he described as an old and almost classic Jewish tendency to look at the outside world with suspicion and mistrust mixed with bitterness and resentment. Particularly noteworthy was his observation that this state of mind is not only prevalent among the older generation and foreign-born Israelis but is also quite typical of the younger and the native-born ones whose personal experiences do not include the traumas of discrimination, persecution and holocaust.

Our keen observer attributes this national psychology to the state of siege under which the people of Israel have been living for the past thirty years, a siege dominated by implacable Arab hostility and a perennial struggle for survival in the most physical sense of the word. "How tragic", he comments, "that this should be the national state of mind in Israel on the eve of the thirtieth anniversary of its independence".

Tragic? Not necessarily. Accurate? Yes. Indeed, when was it any different? Here are some thoughts on this same subject which the writer of these lines expressed before an American audience — on April 29, 1971 — exactly seven years ago, on the eve of Israel's twenty-third anniversary.

Among the other things for which we have been castigated is our isolation. "How come" — we are asked —
"a people as smart as you is so alone in the world?" I
don't know whether we are as smart as all that, but I do
plead guilty to the charge of being alone. This we are
and this we have always been.

At the very dawn of our people, Abraham parted
with his kith and kin and set off by himself for an
unknown land and an uncertain future, not to append
himself to anyone, but to beget a new nation, unlike any
other — a lonely nation bound by covenant to one God.
Three generations later, when it was time for the name
"Israel" to be handed down, it was to be as an award to
the third of the biblical Patriarchs, for having stood the
test of a nocturnal wrestling with an angel of God — the
first of many lonely and arduous trials that Israel was to
endure through the ages. Then came that awesome day
of choice: God and People choosing each other and
pledging eternal allegiance to one another. "Now therefore if ye will obey my voice indeed and keep my covenant"— said God to his chosen people — "then ye shall
be a peculiar people, a treasure unto me above all
peoples. And all the people answered together and said:
All that the Lord hath spoken we will do".

By the time the People of Israel were ready to take
possession of the land God had promised to Abraham,
their peculiarity was sufficiently stamped on them to
enable Balaam — that part-time foreign prophet — to
make the following profound observation, after taking
but one look at them: "From the top of the rocks I see

11

him and from the hills I behold him. Lo the people shall dwell alone and shall not be reckoned among the nations". There it was, stamped on us for all time: a peculiar people dwelling in loneliness among the nations, a loneliness freely contracted as part of a perpetual covenant between them and their God.

And so it has remained through centuries of trial and flourishing, holocaust and triumph. Always alone: Alone they went to the stake in Spain, alone they walked into the gas chambers of Europe. Alone they fought and died in the Warsaw Ghetto. And then, in an act of supreme desperation and faith, alone they retrieved their ancient homeland where once they had dwelt alone.

The genesis of Israel's uniqueness, peculiarity and loneliness hardly began in 1948 but rather dates back to the very dawn of our people some thirty-six centuries ago. Everything that has happened to them since has only served to strengthen and fortify this condition. Israel's national experience since the re-establishment of Jewish independence in the ancient and never-abandoned homeland has hardly been an exception. Ever since its inception the country and the people of Israel have been under constant threat and attack by a host of enemies determined to inflict upon the reborn Jewish nation-state the same fate which so many Jews had come to experience individually in their own wanderings across the time and space expanses of the Diaspora. There was to be no safety for Jews even within the shelter of a Jewish state. Zionism, which took over the torch of Jewish survival just in time before Jewishness was dealt what was to have been a mortal blow, now became the lightning rod for all those for whom the spectacle of Jewish existence is not merely an intriguing phenomenon but the object of a wide range of sentiments ranging from frustration to bestiality. With antisemitism having accomplished its objectives of reducing Jewish existence to "reasonable proportions" — which in certain countries came to mean extinction — it was now possible to swear allegiance to philosemitism, while continuing to labor in the old cause under the new code name of anti-Zionism. Thus for example it has recently been contended that killing Israeli Jews in Israel is less reprehensible than killing Jews elsewhere. Strategically speaking of course all this is sound policy: The eradication of the Zionist state of Israel must in historical terms lead to the annihilation of the Jewish people.

These are sombre thoughts for as festive a season as the forthcoming celebration of the thirtieth anniversary of Israel's independence. And yet it is inevitable that such times be also the occasion for stocktaking. This is particularly appropriate considering the circumstances in which Israel marks this event.

For several months now Israel has been the subject of almost unprecedented criticism and censure. It seems at times as if she could do no right anymore. Every action and non-action, every step, every pronouncement, anything and everything is now the cause and — more often than not — the pretext for an endless barrage of criticism and abuse. A generous peace plan — the first ever to be put forward by any Israeli government — is first described as "fair" and within a fortnight dismissed as unworthy while the absence of any Egyptian proposals or counter-proposals is the subject of no reproach; an Israeli military

13

operation against concentrations of terrorists fresh from their "heroic" offensive against a busload of Israeli civilians and which, not unlike other military operations in history (remember the British bombing of V-1 sites in The Hague?), involves civilian casualties and damage to property, is described in almost genocidal terms; a healthy, sound and open national debate in Israel is heralded as a revolution in the making and a democratically elected government of Israel is almost daily dismissed from office by the ever more sanctimonious media. Nothing is overlooked, nothing missed! An almost impeccable record on human rights is ignored and instead headlines are posted in the newspapers over the marginal reference in a recent American report to "excessive physical force in dispersing demonstrations"; a legitimate effort to put an end to a minor-scale practice of offering financial payments in return for religious conversion is pounced upon as a demonstration of religious intolerance and is immediately made the subject of a detailed and distorted television documentary! And no pretext is necessary for a re-run of a 1975 television documentary on the Middle East of three hours' duration which could serve as a model for malicious and specious news coverage. All this and more in an atmosphere that would seem to suggest that nothing else was happening in the world.

But why all of this? Because Israel has dared to make a number of proposals aimed at providing for a slightly wider margin of security for itself than the verbal or written assurances of the Egyptians would make possible or which would result from the guarantees of others who must know best the limits of their ability or intention to live up to them. The West can insist — and rightly so — on

14

every possible security device in its relations with the East, while Israel is expected to abandon all its earthly possessions in return for promises. The West is free to declare — as did the British Foreign Secretary last week — "Detente — Yes. Peace at any price — No!" while for Israel to say so would earn it the sharpest criticism in the capitals of that same West and the most violent condemnation by all their media. The world's most persecuted and threatened people is called upon to throw caution to the winds, put its trust in everybody who should demand it, give up its defenses and compromise its most basic security, accept and acquiesce in the vast arming of all of its neighbours by every conceivable arms supplier and then patiently wait and see if the horrible security risks undertaken in doing all this were justified! And all this *not* in the stable climate of Western Europe but in the world's most volatile and contested area in which the overwhelming majority of the regimes are still committed to erasing Israel from its map. When Israel dares to say that it is willing to accept *some* of these risks but not all, it is almost declared a pariah, which in the final analysis is yet another good reason why Israel can never, never commit the fatal folly of being lured into accepting the risks demanded of it.

Sombre thoughts on Independence Day? Not necessarily. Just fitting reminders of the realities of our lonely existence and peculiar saga, which we never dare disregard or belittle. But enough of loneliness; I wish to end on another theme equally noteworthy — in my eyes at least — that of friendship. We are indeed in many ways, as God served notice on Abraham, a peculiar people and a lonely one as the perspicacious Balaam diagnosed us. But we are not friendless, certainly not in this country. All one has to do to verify this is to forget the media for a brief moment and establish contact with the *people* all over this country. There he will find, as I have been fortunate to do these past few weeks, a most heartening friendship for Israel and its people, a deep and genuine concern for its future and an unshakable confidence in the justice of its cause. And it is these wonderful people I have been privileged to meet these past days whom I wish to salute on this thirtieth anniversary of Israel's independence.

On Settlements

The Hague, October 28, 1977

It has been said that if the Arab countries were ever to submit a resolution at the United Nations claiming that the world was flat, they could count on the automatic support of at least forty states. Today they seem to have been able to recruit the obeisance of at least seventy states, which is as many as have consented to co-sponsor the Egyptian-inspired resolution on the subject of Israeli settlements in Judea, Samaria and other areas administered by Israel since 1967. No amount of additional support which the resolution stands to gain by the time it is actually voted upon, will detract from its being nothing more than another ploy designed to distract public attention from what regrettably continues to be the heart of the Middle East problem: The refusal of the Arab states to address themselves to the task of achieving true and meaningful peace *between themselves and Israel,* and not merely a "just and lasting peace in the Middle East" — the terminology so religiously touted by them in their effort to evade this critical issue and challenge.

In lending support to this resolution, service is rendered *not* to the cause of peace in the Middle East but rather to yet another sterile skirmish in the constant and unremitting political warfare being waged by the Arab countries in the United Nations, for some years now a central arena for the vilification of Israel.

17

As regards the issue of settlements itself, the following extract from a statement on the subject by Miss Rita E. Hauser, former United States Representative to the United Nations Human Rights Commission, before the International Relations Subcommittee on the Middle East and International Organizations of the United States House of Representatives on September 21, 1977, should help dismiss some distortions and clear up certain misconceptions. Commenting on the key questions of whether the settlements constitute a violation of article 49 of the Fourth Geneva Convention Miss Hauser concludes:

1. Settlements established and run by the military for security purposes, even involving use of the Nahal pioneer youth, is a lawful action by the occupying power in the exercise of its rights to assure the defense and tranquility of the area. They are not intended to be permanent and the local population has rarely been displaced to any serious extent.

2. Settlements in areas over which Israel expects and intends to gain sovereignty in a peace conference can also be viewed as lawful. These settlements are intended to assure the ultimate security interests of Israel. They, too, have rarely involved major displacements of the local population. Compensation has been paid or tendered for the land.

3. As to the third type of settlement in areas heavily populated by Arabs, to the extent the settlements were private in nature and unsanctioned by the Israel Government, there is nothing in international law which would render them unlawful. Whether or not they violate applicable local law is another matter.

Legalization of certain of these settlements by the Israel Government, however, brings them within the purview of Article 49 of the Fourth Geneva Convention. Israel has not, to date, extended Israeli law to these settlements, refraining thus from annexing them. Rather, Israel maintains the settlements may well remain in place after a peace treaty even if the territories in question are awarded to the relevant Arab belligerent. Pending such event, a given Jewish settlement in an occupied area may satisfy Article 49. The relevant issue is whether or not the local population has been displaced in the course of establishing the settlement.

I would therefore conclude that, to date, the three types of settlements in the occupied territories on the whole do not violate article 49 of the Fourth Geneva Convention. The displacement of the local population was minimal in all cases: compensation for the permanent settlements was paid or tendered; the total number of Israelis who have settled is small (about 3,000).

If extensive settlement throughout the occupied territories were to occur, involving serious displacement of the local population and the movement into the area by a substantial number of Israelis, then it could well be argued that Israel would have violated not only article 49, but the very premise on which a belligerent occupancy is viewed under international law. At a certain point, which I believe has not yet been anywhere near reached, occupancy would shade over into annexation or quasi-annexation.

While the Arabs may complain bitterly about this situation, the underlying reality is that an occupying power will not forever stay frozen in that posture. The law of belligerent occupancy presupposes a short duration pending the calling of a peace conference. Had such a peace conference occurred by now, this whole issue would be moot.

At some point in time, as a practical matter, an annexation process will replace the normal end product of diplomacy, which is a peace treaty. The refusal to negotiate a peace treaty on the part of the Arab countries, enunciated by them at Khartoum in the fall of 1967, has led to this anomalous situation which only enlightened politics can now resolve.

One final note: Jewish presence in the Land of Israel has been constant and uninterrupted since the dawn of the People of Israel. No other nation can claim this unique relationship between people and country. As for Jewish *settlement* in Eretz Israel it is as old as the Patriarch Abraham's *settlement* there some thirty-seven centuries ago. And it too has been just as uninterrupted throughout these past three and a half millennia. The notion that Judea and Samaria, of all places, should be out of bounds to Jews — literally Judenrein — is quite frankly blasphemous and certainly unacceptable to Israel. Nevertheless, Israel's policy on the question of settlements was enunciated by Foreign Minister Moshe Dayan from the rostrum of the United Nations on October 10, 1977 as follows:

The settlements will not decide the final borders between Israel and its neighbours. The borders will be decided upon in negotiations between Israel and its neighbours.

The Arab countries have only to come forward and test Israel on this through open and direct negotiations with it. All other parties would also render a service to the cause of peace if they were to direct their efforts towards this central objective.

Israel — The Jewish Backyard?

Remarks at
the Meeting of the Board of Deputies of British Jews
Bournemouth, February 1, 1981

The World Jewish Congress has just met in Jerusalem. One of the items on the agenda was a Report on Israel-Diaspora relations prepared by an international panel of distinguished Jews, mostly businessmen and financiers, including a number of Israelis.

Following are some salient quotations from the "Report" as cited by the Press.

> The classic Zionist ideology which denigrates the pros-pects for a secure or meaningful Jewish existence in the Diaspora and which conceives of Diaspora existence as living in exile is remote from the thinking of most Jews who live in fully democratic societies.
>
> The persistent hopes and efforts of Zionist organiza-tions to increase immigration from *Western* Diaspora communities cannot confidently be counted upon to achieve far greater successes than they have in the past.

This ideology "is not conducive to effective communica-tion between Israelis and emancipated secular Diaspora Jews".

Criticism of Israel's domestic and foreign policies by Jews should not be "swept under the rug" but openly expressed in order to relieve "increasing strains" in the relationship between Israel and the Diaspora. The right to differ with Israel was "by far the most important of outstanding current issues" between Israel and the Diaspora.

Israel itself is depicted by the Report as a society whose hallmarks include the following:

"...extremely parochial obtuseness of settlement policy";

"...intensely fragmented, fractional, contentious, unstable and generally unseemly political scene."

"...flawed electoral system incapable of resolving basic issues."

"...growing materialism that has hastened the erosion of the old ideas and Jewish values centering on the idea of social justice."

"...religious monopoly exercised by the orthodox rabbinate in Israel."

These are some of the ingredients of modern Israel as portrayed by the World Jewish Congress Report. They were complemented by some of the remarks made by the new President of the Congress, Mr. Edgar Bronfman, in his acceptance speech: "The Jews of the Diaspora should not be expected blindly to support the Government of Israel in every single matter. Automatic rigid adherence to every position of the Government can be ineffective in influencing our own Governments outside of Israel." While Israel is of central importance "it is not the only item nor should it be" on the agenda of the Diaspora. "As citizens of their own countries Jews must and should be concerned with the affairs, the economic, moral and political climate of those countries where they live."

In an interview which he later gave to the *Jerusalem Post* Mr. Bronfman also had this to say: "It is a mistake for

Israel or for Israelis to make the Diaspora feel guilty for not making 'aliya'. I am trying to be practical. I do not think my children or grandchildren will ever move to Israel."

Taken together, these quotations from the Report and from some of the statements that have been made in conjunction with it would seem to project the following concept of Israel and Israel-Diaspora relations:

There is really nothing very special about the Jewish state of Israel which entitles it to any priority, precedence or privilege vis-à-vis the rest of the Jewish world. Such notions about the centrality of Israel in the Jewish world are a relic of "classic" — i.e. old, archaic — Zionism. They have no place in the present and they have no prospect for the future. The children of Jewish leaders will not come to Israel and neither should they be expected to. Israel in effect has no claim to more than parity with its sister communities. It may have a flag and a government and an army but these are not very much more than idiosyncrasies and constitute no special claim to glory. Israelis therefore have no right to expect Western Diaspora Jews to come and join them nor is there any justification for it.

Moreover, Israel really has not very much to offer Western Diaspora olim — as distinct of course from *non*-Western Diaspora olim. Look at the state it is in. Its society is a shambles, its political system a disgrace. It is plagued with materialism and its ideal of social justice has been eroded. What justification does it have for demanding of Jews to come — unless they still be fired by that fossilized, archaic, primitive, passé notion of Zionism? What is more, Israelis have no right to complain. This privilege is apparently reserved exclusively for those Jews who reside outside the confines of the Jewish state. They have the right to criticise and censure Israel and to lament its failings, and unless they are given that right, grievous damage will be done to Israel-Diaspora relations. Such is apparently the state and the status of Israel according to the World Jewish Congress and those who subscribe to its views.

If this be the case then some very serious questions arise and others gain credence: Why a Jewish state, if the Jews themselves do not consider it central to their individual and communal lives? Why a Jewish community with the full trappings of a state when it has no more claim to distinction than any other community? Surely not for the sake of such things as a flag and an army? An army is a deadly business anyway. Why a Jewish state if such are its failings? Why a Jewish state if it is deserving of such criticism — not only from the non-Jewish media which have their reasons for taking Israel to task but also from its own kith and kin?

Others may be emboldened to ask why *such* a Jewish state at such cost to international prosperity and stability. Why should those countries that still do so, continue to exert themselves in support of Israel and its rights, if it is considered to have no more claim on Jews than to that limited degree suggested by the World Jewish Congress? And still others may seize upon such a concept of Israel in order to hoist and hang their brand of question mark over Israel: Why a Jewish state which has no more claim or right than any one of the other Jewish communities? Why not another Jewish community within a democratic secular republic similar to Jewish communities elsewhere?

Render Israel a run-of-the-mill Jewish collective, and a

25

lacklustre one at that, and yet another question might be raised. Why fight for this kind of country? Why shed blood for it, if it is not the centre of the Jewish world and the central theme of Jewish life? Why die for it if it is the expression of no more than an archaic, obsolete and fossilized idea? This in turn may raise yet another question: If Israel is but another Jewish community possessed of no uniqueness and devoid of any majesty and on a par with any of its sister communities, then why should young Israelis be expected to continue to attach themselves to it at such risk to their lives, and when it is deserving of such censure and criticism as is meted out by no less a personage than the President of the World Jewish Congress? Why should they not pack their bags and move to within a mile of where the President of the World Jewish Congress lives to drive a taxi out there, as some already do? Why should they differ from other young Jews at a time when Jews are on the move again: South Africans are moving. Latin Americans are moving. Russians are moving. Why should Israeli youngsters be denied this freedom of mobility? If not coming to Israel is no grounds for even regret, then why should quitting it be so? Why cannot Israel's young people also pack up and move to join another Jewish community where life is so much more comfortable, where one does not have to shed blood, where one can live happily ever after and be entitled to the same rights and privileges and distinction? And why should bright young Israelis, just as bright as those of Park Avenue — maybe even brighter — have to spend four years in the army? Why not go straight into business on Park Avenue?

It is as simple and as brutal as that: If Zionism is as obsolete and as irrelevant as is suggested by the World

Jewish Congress then so is the Jewish state. Destroy Zionism and you have destroyed the state. Moreover there is no meaning to Zionism unless it is predicated on "aliya" *including* the right to criticise people for not responding to its challenge. Zionism and its synonym "aliya" are the only prerogative Israelis *must* insist upon. No more, no less. And let no one deny us the right — if we should wish to exercise it — to criticise Jews for not coming to join with us in our present difficult circumstances and in our struggle and hope for better times.

But what of Israel? Does it really deserve to be portrayed as that gloomy picture of failure which emerges from some of the statements made at the recent World Jewish Congress meeting? Have we Israelis failed in our job and betrayed the trust put in us, or is Israel a magnificent story of achievement? Could it be that we have really acquitted ourselves above and beyond all expectations?

Have we failed to protect Israel physically? Have we failed to repel the constant aggression waged against it for thirty-two years? Have we lost an inch? Have we given up a yard? Is Jerusalem still a divided city? Is the country wide open to marauders and terrorists? Is it defenceless and at the mercy of its enemies or rather a powerful and invincible fortress?

Have we failed to absorb those Jews who have come to our shores? Have we failed to provide them with a haven, and was not this the primary goal and raison d'être of Israel? Did not the state come into being as a result of a struggle for "aliya"? Did we not take on the entire British Empire and challenge an armada of ships and hosts of troops only for the sake of bringing in the refugees and the immigrants? Was this not the cause we fought for?

27

Have we turned away a single Jew since? Have we said "no" to any Jew because he was penniless? Have we closed our doors to Jews because they were not healthy, either in mind or in body or because they were blind or maimed or decrepit? Have we passed these Jews on to other more affluent communities in order to avoid being burdened by the cost of restoring them to good health or maintaining them if that were not possible? Did we select only the young and the able-bodied and reject the old and infirm, as others might have done in circumstances such as ours? We have *not* done so; nor would it ever have occurred to us. We have taken all the maimed, the sick, the ill, the demented, the blind and the crippled of whom there were masses, and many of those were unloaded on us as others more fit went elsewhere. And today some people have the temerity to complain about our blemishes!

Have we failed to build a country? Is Israel the desert that it once was or is it the scene of one of the world's most remarkable agricultural revolutions? Turning a desert into a blossoming garden has become a cliché but that does not detract from the achievement: We said we would return to the land and we did. We said we would revive the land and we did. We said we would make the land blossom and we did. But we have not only converted Jews into farmers after thousands of years of absence from the land. We have also put them to work in factories, laboratories, workshops, all of which today combine to make Israel's industry one of the technologically and scientifically most advanced in the world. We do not only produce avocados, we also produce scanners along with supersonic planes, sophisticated optical equipment, the finest textiles, chemicals, machinery, and more. And we have also developed an

28

extraordinary educational infrastructure which annually produces the brains required for the manning of this remarkable manufacturing complex which is Israel's industry.

Have we failed to live up to the highest traditions of Jewish learning? Is Israel not the scene of the most intense intellectual and cultural activity? Have we ceased to be a "people of the book"? Do we not publish more books per capita than most book-reading countries? Do we not annually graduate more students than practically any other country our size? Is our music substandard and our theatre stale?

Have we betrayed our democratic tradition? Is Israel no longer an open and free society? Do we change governments by coups d'état or is not the will of the people — freely expressed and democratically applied — the true and decisive determinant of policy and of government?

Above all have we not been good and loyal and true to our Jewish brethren? Have we turned our backs to our fellow Jews? Have we not opened our hearts to them? Do we criticise them for not coming on "aliya"? Do we embarrass them publicy for not doing so? Do we even bear them a grudge for failing us? We do none of these things. Those who come are welcome. Those who do not come are no less welcome.

And yet it is suggested that there is a strain in the present Israel-Diaspora relations. Moreover, it is claimed that this strain is the result of lack of opportunity or allowance for criticism of Israel by Western Diaspora Jews. It is even argued that the central issue of our times is whether or not Jews will be able to criticise Israel to their heart's content. This will apparently make or break Jewish-Diaspora relations. This no less is the great challenge presently facing the Jewish world. As if there is peace along all of Israel's borders. As if the state is finally secure. As if the country's continuing economic and social problems — which are in great part the price tag for unrestricted "aliya" — have been resolved. And as if, on the other hand, the dangers of assimilation in the Western Diaspora are a figment of someone's imagination. As if every Jewish child in the West receives full Jewish education. As if commitment to Jewish ethics is the hallmark of Diaspora Jewish life. And, yes, as if there is a constant stream of "olim" from the West to Israel.

To suggest that an alleged lack of opportunities for Diaspora criticism of Israel — as if that were the most pressing Jewish need of our times — is the cause of a major strain in Israel-Diaspora relations is a total misreading of the Jewish condition today, revealing a profound ignorance of the prerequisites and essentials of Jewish survival.

Finally, a word of caution: We Israelis are not perfect and we are not without blemish and no one knows better than we how serious some of our problems are. Let nobody, however, entertain any illusions about our willingness to subject ourselves to a barrage of flagellation from people whose commitment to Israel is best reflected by a public announcement that neither they nor their children will ever come to live there. Life in Israel is not easy. It involves constant effort and much sacrifice. It costs lives and consumes precious and scant assets. Sometimes it also involves deep anguish. Let no one add to our burdens, especially when there is no cause nor reason for doing so. We have not been remiss in our dedication to our people. We have not failed in our commitment to our cause. We are *not* a Jewish backyard. *We are the heart and soul of the Jewish world. Without Israel there is no Jewish future.* Let no one therefore tamper with our pride as Israelis. One of these days we may decide that we are not willing to continue to put up with such things as are being said to us and about us at meetings of the World Jewish Congress.

On Peace and Security: Perceptions and Principles of Israeli Policy

*A lecture given at the Royal United Services Institute
for Defence Studies (RUSI)
London, January 27, 1982*

To be able to defend oneself by oneself in this day and age is generally a luxury reserved only for superpowers. Apart from the United States and the Soviet Union, hardly any country presumes or seeks to maintain such capability. Europe has long abandoned any such presumptions. European defence today is a joint American-European venture given effect and symbol by a massive American military presence in Western Europe and the protection of America's nuclear umbrella. Against all apparent logic little Israel insists on demanding for itself that which others, much bigger, much richer and much more populous have long given up. This is not a result of national vanity or of an inflated perception of prowess. Rather it is a function of Israel's unique strategic vulnerability. Being able to defend itself by itself is Israel's only possible answer to its unparalleled security problem.

In essence the strategic challenge which Israel faces consists of the need to contend with four major disparities: the disparity of geography, the disparity of demography

* Reprinted with permission from the *RUSI Journal,* June 1982.

and economics, the disparity of arms and the disparity of intent.

Disparity of Geography

Israel is a tiny country bedevilled by enormous boundary lines. Until 1967 it had no strategic depth to speak of. Jerusalem — Israel's capital — was for 19 years within easy sniper range and twice within that period was heavily shelled by Jordanian artillery. Tel-Aviv — Israel's largest city — was until 1967 only eleven miles away from the old armistice lines and in 1967 was also shelled by Jordanian guns. The entire coastal plain of Israel, where over 60% of the country's population live and work, is roughly at a similar distance from the old line. At one point near the seaside city of Netanya that line was just nine miles away.

Today the defence of Israel's "eastern approaches" is anchored in the north in the Golan Heights and to the south in the Jordan Valley Rift and the eastern slopes and ridges of Judea and Samaria. The distances, however, continue to remain minuscule. At Israel's widest point the Mediterranean is only fifty-one miles away from the Jordan, while at its narrowest the sea is a mere twenty-eight miles away from the river. In the north it is still possible to fire a long-range artillery shell from Syrian territory right across the Golan Heights and the Huleh Valley into Lebanese territory on the other side! Such is the measure of Israel's stategic depth today. In practical military terms this means that a successful armoured thrust from the present eastern lines can cut Israel in half in a matter of hours while a similarly successful effort from the 1967 lines

33

could have achieved this objective literally in a matter of minutes. In a part of this tiny area roughly the size of Wales, with borders twice as long as those of Wales, it is nowadays often proposed to plant a Palestinian state run and led by an organization which openly declares its intention to use such a state as a forward base from which, at an opportune time, to lead a final assault on the remainder of Israel.

The Demographic-Economic Disparity

Israel's geographic vulnerability is compounded by a vast demographic disparity which in turn is made more acute by an even greater economic disadvantage. All told there are barely three and a half million Israelis while the combined population of the Arab world is close to 150 million. As for economic resources, Saudi Arabia's annual GNP alone is four times greater than Israel's. This demographic-economic disparity means that the Arab countries can with little effort maintain very large standing armies — which is precisely what they do. The total number of Arab forces — excluding Egypt — is presently put at 1,245,000 troops. These are full-time combat-trained soldiers ready to move at short notice.

Israel for its part cannot maintain a standing army of any consequence. Its immediately available fighting force consists of the national servicemen of the day plus a relatively small complement of career officers and NCOs. The bulk of Israel's army is made up of reservists who in an emergency must be converted from civilians into fighting soldiers within a matter of hours. On Yom Kippur 1973, many Israelis found themselves on the battlefield within

34

some six to seven hours of leaving home or synagogue. Efficient as Israel's call-up system may be, it involves a frightening degree of risk. Its success, on which the country's very survival depends, requires a minimal time-frame within which the call-up can be effected. Allowing for this time-frame is the responsibility of the young national servicemen whose task it is to hold the line long enough for their elder brothers, and very often also their fathers, to rush from home and work to their respective depots, there to pick up their arms, equipment and fighting vehicles and on into battle. In the final analysis this immensely complicated and hazardous enterprise stands or falls by the initial opening phase.

Had the 1973 war started from the 1967 lines, this discussion today would not be taking place. There would have been nothing left to discuss or to explain and most likely very few Israelis with whom to do so even as a post-mortem. And yet today there are many who would have us go back to the tortuous, indefensible lines of 1967, though these have been rendered by now literally absurd as a result of the introduction of yet another massive constraint in the form of the enormous military build-up which has taken place in the Arab world in recent years and which continues unabated.

The Disparity of Arms

The Arab world today possesses the largest arsenal of arms and armaments outside the United States and the Soviet Union, exceeding the collective military strength of Western Europe. Consider the figures for armour: the combined armoured strength of the Arab world today —

35

excluding Egypt — is put at over 14,000 tanks. By comparison the total number of tanks at the disposal of NATO is some 17,000. In other words the Arabs — excluding Egypt — have almost as many tanks as NATO and almost half the number of tanks which the Soviet Union is known to have deployed west of the Urals. These Soviet tanks, we are told, present the gravest conventional Soviet military threat to Western European defence. So much so in fact as to create the need for non-conventional redressive measures such as the neutron bomb. And yet a nation of three and a half million people is somehow expected to meet an Arab armoured force almost half as big as the Soviet armoured force facing Europe by pulling back from its present relatively defensible lines to ones for which no military High Command would dare assume responsibility in similar circumstances anywhere.

The magnitude and significance of these figures may perhaps be made even more stark by the following comparative statistics: the combined number of tanks on both sides in the battle of El-Alamein in 1942 was 1,518 tanks — 1,029 British and 489 German. At the end of the battle 460 German tanks were destroyed or knocked out at the cost of some 500 British tanks. By contrast, in the Yom Kippur War of 1973, the Syrians alone struck with upwards of 1,500 tanks. By the end of the battle four days later, 1,150 Syrian tanks had been destroyed. (The tank ratio on the Golan Heights during the opening phases of the campaign was one Israeli tank to ten Syrian tanks.)

These statistics do not convey the full picture considering the immense difference in quality between today's tanks and their 1942 equivalent. There is no comparing the Soviet T-62 and T-72 with Rommel's Tigers or the British

Chieftain (certainly not the version which has recently been sold to Jordan) with Montgomery's Shermans, Grants and Crusaders of the Eighth Army. Today Syrian armour alone is estimated at 3,700 tanks, an increasing number of which, indeed many hundreds by now, are T-72s — the most advanced tank in the Soviet arsenal. This is the tank which the future British Challenger, the American XM-1 and the present German Leopard II are designed to counteract. Israel's answer to the T-72 is its own Merkava battle-tank.

Such an awesome recitation of figures normally elicits either of the following two retorts or both. First, there is the standard argument that all this is "old hat" and that ours is the age of ICBMs, not of tanks, rendering such factors as armoured vehicles and ground distances of no consequence. To those who argue so we would suggest that they take note of the desperate efforts to conventionalise future warfare or at the very least to limit its nuclearisation. We would also beg to offer the thought that the last thing the Middle East and the rest of the world need is for the Middle East also to begin to talk in ICBM terms. The dimensions and perils of conventional warfare in the Middle East are harrowing enough.

The other frequent retort is that the remedy to the agonies of the Middle East is not more weapons but more peace. This we heartily endorse. But that still leaves a "slight" problem which has to do with the fourth of the disparities with which Israel has to contend.

The Disparity of Intent

There is nothing Israelis desire more than peace. To suggest or to suspect otherwise is to malign us no end. Not

37

only has Israel everything to gain from peace — as incidentally do the Arabs — but it has also proven itself capable of making enormous sacrifices and concessions for the sake of peace. One of the many perversions of war however, is that it normally takes place between countries hitherto at peace with each other. Not only is the Middle East not exempt from this strange anomaly but it will be a long time before the region is at peace with itself. Suffice it to recall how the recent Arab summit in Fez broke up because of inability to agree on a Saudi formula which included a reference to "the right of all countries of the region to live in peace" for fear that others would stretch this to mean that in certain circumstances it could be inferred to apply also to Israel.

When the peace millennium does finally arrive it will still leave Israel with the problem of living at the very least with a dormant Arab propensity to break the peace. Just as it is inconceivable that Israel would ever wish to attack any of its neighbours even in the absence of blissful peace, so is it quite conceivable that one or more of its neighbours may at any time — either by deliberate and calculated design or as a result of an abrupt internal upheaval — suddenly turn against Israel and sweep others less aggressively inclined along with them. This is the disparity of intent with which Israel also has to contend and the one that makes the need for vigilance a permanent feature of Israel's national life.

These are the disparities with which Israel had to cope until now and with which it will always have to live. Added together they dictate a defence doctrine predicated on one harsh and exacting principle: given the minuscule distances, the overwhelming Arab preponderance in numbers and armaments and the prospect of continued Arab malevolence into the distant future, the only power in which Israel can afford to entrust its security is Israel itself. Only Israel can provide for its defence against a surprise onslaught, for it alone can respond with the instinct, speed, decisiveness and existential commitment required to prevent national catastrophe. To do so effectively, however, Israel must have at least minimal geographic assets to counter the disparity of geography; maximal effective utilisation of its limited manpower resources in order to match the disparity of demography and economics; a minimal qualitative edge to make up for the disparity of arms, and maximal intelligence capability with which to balance the disparity of intent.

This is why it would be advisable for friend and foe alike to realise that there is a limit to what can be demanded of Israel even for the sake of peace. And to those who would say to us that unless we pull back to the 1967 lines and permit the establishment of a PLO state — which is what the Venice Declaration effectively calls for — we are doomed to continue to live by the sword, we would suggest that they ponder the practical applications of similar advice in European circumstances.

Applied to the European scene the practical equivalent of what is demanded of Israel is the following: the dismantling of NATO; the withdrawal of American troops from Western Europe; the removal of Polaris submarines from European waters; the exclusion of B-52s from European skies, entrusting the freedom of Europe to the goodwill and faith of the Soviet Union and allowing for the establishment of little East Germanies in the heart of every Western European country. That in strategic terms is the equivalent of what is demanded of us by, for example, the protagonists of Venice. Those who demand this of Israel have either not consulted their military chiefs, which is careless, or else do not feel obliged to concern themselves with the certain consequences of the fulfilment of their demands, and that is rash. Not that it is the first time.

In 1938 another reborn nation was coerced into removing itself from its lines of defence in order to allow for a process of self-determination for a certain population which protruded into its territory. Within six months that country ceased to exist when it could very well have been able to hold its own if only it were able to continue to man those lines of defence which it was pressured to abandon. We cannot commit such folly. The Czechs could disappear as a free state and survive as a nation, not only once but three times running — in 1938, 1948 and 1968. If our state goes under, all of us go under and along with us a national odyssey extending over more than four millennia. This we are sworn not to permit to happen.

Hence, if you wish, our compulsive obsession with defence which is certain to remain permanent and indelible. A unique historical experience has ensured that. Hence our resolve to obtain for ourselves new lines offering more security than the old fragile and indefensible ones of 1967.

This hardly promises to be a popular exercise for it is apparently far more permissible for a member-state of the United Nations to insist on implacable, eternal enmity towards Israel than for Israel to draw a line behind which to brace and protect itself against such openly declared aggression. It was nevertheless strange to be told in the

Security Council — as we recently were — that, "If Israel by such actions continues to distance herself further from accommodation with her neighbours she cannot expect to escape the consequences indefinitely". Pray, what "accommodation" and with which "neighbour"? Can those who have spoken so harshly point to the slightest indication of a desire for "accommodation" — any "accommodation" — by that same Syria which was offered these words of succour? No less strange — for us at least — was the whole experience of being hauled before the Security Council to account for our sins as that same Council continued to hold its peace while two of its members — including a "permanent" one — continued to make a mockery of every norm and practice of international behaviour. A special touch of cynicism was added when these two countries, i.e. the Soviet Union and Poland, enthusiastically joined in supporting a draft resolution calling for voluntary sanctions against Israel.

We have also been told at the same Security Council debate that the "...patience of the international community has been sorely tried". But what of our patience? For months on end Israel has been subjected to a barrage of statements and pronouncements — from "Venice" to "Riyadh" — spelling out precisely how far it should withdraw and what should be its borders. It is entirely unrealistic to expect Israel to be told and retold all this while continuing to exercise limitless patience and not to ripost and publicly delineate where it believes and intends its future boundaries to be. Moreover, while these calls for total Israeli withdrawal to the 1967 lines run against the letter and spirit of Resolution 242, there is nothing in that

Resolution to prevent Israel from insisting on and striving for new and secure boundaries. There would have been no Resolution 242 had this been the case.

One essential point needs to be understood: the spectacle of total Israeli withdrawal, as from the Sinai peninsula, will not be repeated elsewhere and it is perhaps important that this should be made clear precisely as this withdrawal is being completed. We are in absolute earnest about our resolve to achieve for ourselves new and viable boundaries. This is the result neither of idiosyncrasy nor the product of irrational whim but rather the dictate of the strategic and historic facts of our lives. Just as these are unique to us so must we claim final say in determining the ways and the means by which to respond to them.

Discussion Following the Ambassador's Lecture

The first question concerned the establishment of the Multinational Peacekeeping Force and Observers (MFO) in Sinai. The Ambassador commented that the purpose of the force is to help ensure as far as possible that Sinai is effectively demilitarised, and to ensure freedom of navigation along the coastal waterways. He continued, "It is in a sense symbolic, but the symbol is very important, above all that of American participation, although we obviously welcome European participation too, as this widens the base. The idea is to ensure that Sinai never again becomes a launching pad from where to strike into Israel and cause antagonism between ourselves and our neighbours to the south. Hopefully, this situation will not occur again, and there will be no need for such a deterrent as this force provides. We base our hopes on continued peace between

Egypt and Israel and hope we are right in believing that it is in the national interest of Egypt to continue to maintain that peace with us. It is that national interest which I think was the basis for the remarkable initiative by President Sadat and we pray that it will continue to be the foundation for future Egyptian policy with regard to its relations with Israel."

On Israel's contribution to the peace process, the Ambassador said, "We made a deal. We signed a document. We entered into a contractual agreement with our Egyptian neighbours which was a contractual agreement also with the sponsor and patron of the entire exercise, namely the United States. We committed ourselves to tackle two problems. One was the direct Egyptian-Israeli relationship. That was taken care of, we believe adequately, by the making of peace. We have however incurred grave risks. Israel did not acquire Sinai as part of a legacy and we do not and have never claimed Sinai because we once spent 40 years there. We stumbled into Sinai and found ourselves in possession as a result of a war of self-defence we neither wanted nor initiated. While we were there, we invested enormous amounts of money and resources in creating in Sinai an infrastructure of defence, all of which we have now scrapped. I think you will appreciate what we are doing. There were economic assets there as well. This is the first time in recent history that a country has given up oil resources. Israel is making an enormous effort for the sake of peace. It was not a mere *quid pro quo*. Egypt made peace and gave us back what they owed us — recognition, coexistence. For years they denied us that. They gave that to us as we gave them the same. Egypt, too, needs peace.

"We gave a great deal more than that. There was another set of commitments to which we are signatory, concerning a problem which is really extraneous to Egyptian-Israeli relations. The Americans insisted on this, and we agreed and accepted the fact that under the Camp David agreements there was a need to make a beginning towards resolving the Palestinian problem. Why have we made no progress since? I think there was not enough support for the Camp David accords. Camp David, instead of becoming the beacon of peace, became instead a dirty word. The whole peace process was tarnished by adverse criticism and lack of support. Had it been given backing, we would have been well on the way towards progress.

"The Venice Declaration was introduced at precisely the time when we needed everything Venice is not. We needed the fullest support for the Camp David principles. Instead, we found ourselves doing battle with an attempt to switch the entire process elsewhere. The Venice Declaration calls for the establishment of a Palestinian state. Nothing in Camp David calls for this. There would have been no Camp David agreements had either of these options been called for. Hence our rejection of the Venice Declaration, and many of its principles. We accept the need for recognition, but which party is being denied recognition? Which party to this day continues to be denied recognition? The Arabs went to Fez in November 1981 not to recognise Israel but to reach agreement on a statement which others might conceivably have inferred as suggesting eventual recognition. The summit broke up within a few hours. They could not agree. Some people think we were pleased that such was the outcome of Fez. In a sense this is true because we knew they were not about to discuss or to agree on recognition, but it was very depressing for Israel to be confronted yet again with the Arab demonstration of rejection, of denunciation, of lack of willingness to come to terms."

The Ambassador was asked to comment on the sometimes acrimonious diplomatic exchanges during the recent past. He said, "It is true harsh words have been exchanged. They were sometimes expressed in the flash of argument and not always meant to be harsh. The past year has been an unhappy one in this respect. I would ask you to see things from Israel's point of view. We were really responding, and some harsh words were a frustrated response to an effort to promote ideas, processes, formulae that really are anathema to Israel. There cannot be a PLO state. If people set about establishing one, the least we can do is to rebel against the idea. If harsh words were said, they are indicative of the sense of great grievance and frustration that we feel.

"You cannot interrupt a process midway. The Egyptian-Israeli peace is only part of the agreement. The Palestinian question which needs to be tackled by the other part of the agreement is binding on us, but in accordance with the Camp David agreements. You cannot come along in the middle and say, 'Now that you have acquitted yourselves so well and pulled out of Sinai, do the rest our way'. No. There was an agreement binding all parties. And that is the one that is binding us, and one we are very anxious to continue to explore."

When asked what the Western countries can do to help Israel, the Ambassador said that a prerequisite for help was understanding. He continued, "Ours has been a fairly lonely journey. I am not referring to the historic one. I am referring to the peacemaking process. We have had to carry an enormous burden and with very little help. And this is really at the heart of the frustration. I think there is need for people to accept what we concede to others, namely, the existence of vital national interests. Just as others have vital national interests, so do we. Given their acuteness, given the precariousness of our position, I think we deserve an extra measure of understanding and support. I think we have the right to ask of people to consider, for example, in a detached military fashion precisely what would happen if Venice ever came into being. How would the little state that would remain of Israel today be able to continue to survive? Now, we have in a very professional military manner dealt with this problem a long time ago. And the conclusion was that we have not the slightest chance of surviving for any length of time if such a scenario were to become a reality. The Venice Declaration included ideas and principles galore, but a serious consideration of the consequences to us has not, I think, really been sufficiently tackled. Europe and the United States have vital interests in the Middle East. We believe those interests are not necessarily in conflict with ours. The existence in the Middle East of a little country by the name of Israel which possesses substantial power and which is an integral part of what we call the free world is not necessarily a liability.

"I would suggest to you that an Israel at peace with Egypt is keeping that part of the Middle East reasonably stable while the rest of the region is disintegrating before our eyes. There is nothing new about this. The Middle East has been in a state of upheaval for years. Look at Syria, Lebanon, Iran, Iraq, the Gulf, South Yemen, North

Yemen, Ethiopia, Somalia, Sudan and Libya. That is the Arab world today. There is but one island of stability there — and that has been created as a result of the Egyptian-Israeli peace process. Israel itself radiates strength and, as a result of that, stability. It is a plucky little country with which one has to come to terms and make peace. I would hate to think of the Middle East today without an Egyptian-Israeli peace programme. And I would hate to think of the Middle East without Israel. There would be no Jordan and quite a few other people would disappear as a result too. We provide a great deal of stability in that part of the world, which is why we believe there is an interest in having a strong Israel rather than a little country that will be totally dependent on the graces of others.

"It is the discord between Israel and Europe and between us and other parties which is causing much damage to the peace process. We are very anxious for harmony between ourselves and our European friends on the question of peace in the Middle East, and if that harmony was forthcoming, I think it would improve the chances of making progress.

"Once we are put to the test of peacemaking we acquit ourselves well. Everything I have said today represents not just government policy but what we call the national consensus, the heart, the core of the thinking of most Israelis. Israeli public opinion is united on the need for a better geographic deployment for the country and its people. Everything I have tried to articulate is common knowledge to all of us in Israel. It is the daily business of Israelis who have to do military reserve duty every year and have to be prepared for an onslaught by all those Arab tanks. They are not going to accept a line from which any attempt to protect Israel against these tanks is doomed. And they know best. They have had to beat back Arab tanks so many times. Those who did it in 1973 in the Golan will be the first to tell you it cannot be done if we ever climb down from the Golan. Had the Syrians succeeded in breaking through in 1973 — and they almost did — and in rushing on to the Huleh Valley and from there to Tiberias and on to the Valley of Jezreel and Haifa then the whole business of call-up and reserves and of attempting to save the country would have collapsed. The whole thing is so fragile. There are just so many roads, just so many access routes, just so much or little space and depth.

"This is why we are so insistent and so adamant, if you wish, about these things. Our concerns may seem outmoded. Everybody else talks in other terms. We talk in these terms because they are the most relevant for us; we live by them and some of us have died by them."

On Things that are Taken for Granted

Speech to the Joint Israel Appeal
Newcastle-upon-Tyne, January 31, 1982

We meet tonight in the cause of Israel. We also meet at an important time in its history, a time when the people of Israel and the State of Israel are bracing themselves for an exacting agenda in the immediate and forseeable future. Confronting us in the coming year are some very important milestones. Some of these are well known to us. There may well be others about which we do not yet know. Come April of this year — barely three months from now — we shall have completed the withdrawal from the Sinai Peninsula — an important and difficult milestone, hardly appreciated by the rest of the world and taken for granted by some of us also. By April 26 of this year we will have pulled out from that expanse of desert which for the past thirteen years has given us more security than we have ever known before and which at a critical moment in the history of the State of Israel enabled its people to repel an enemy which struck suddenly and which threatened to do us grievous damage. The ability of Israel to withdraw into that desert so as to be able to raise its army in defence of the land and the people was crucial to the ultimate triumph of the Yom Kippur War. Had we not had that desert we might have had to fall back not on the wastes of Sinai but on the towns and villages of the south of Israel. That margin of safety the Sinai offered us we now give up.

49

Along with giving up the Sinai Peninsula and an enormous strategic infrastructure as well as unique economic assets, we are also experiencing something that we have never known before: we are uprooting ourselves. We are uprooting people, hamlets, homes, towns, villages, factories and fields. This we have never done before and it is a doubly traumatic experience for people whose whole life has revolved around the concept of settling the land. In Sinai these days we are unsettling the land. This is the experience which is presently rocking the society and body politic of Israel, causing anguish to a great many of its people.

All this should not be taken for granted: we are not simply living up to our commitments as we have undertaken to do. We are going through a veritable ordeal for the sake of what we consider to be a great prize worthy and deserving, even of such sacrifice — peace! A peace we have fought for, longed for and prayed for. A peace with a country until not so very long ago Israel's foremost enemy and with which we have had to do battle no less than five times. And it was the will and the wish and the decision of the people of Israel — democratically arrived at and democratically determined — that peace has first priority and deserves all of the sacrifices and all of the risks required for its consummation. We hope — indeed, we *pray* — that we shall not ever have reason to regret having made this decision and that April 26 will not be a cut-off date after which things will begin to unravel but rather a date that will be followed by further progress towards the creation of neighbourly, peaceful relations with the people of Egypt.

And so we look beyond April 26. As we do so, however,

we should also do well not to lose our historical perspec-
tive, especially since we are somewhat prone to take things
for granted. It is today accepted as perfectly normal and
natural by all of us that there should be a State of Israel —
which is right and as it should be. There is and there will
always be an Israel. And yet barely thirty-four years ago
there was no state, no Jewish independence, and no sovereign home for the Jewish people. Indeed there were no
such things as Israeli Ambassadors. If you wish, the
manner in which we have come to take all these for granted
is the measure of our fantastic success. It has thus become
second nature for us to accept miraculous things as the
most obvious and natural in the world. But then it was not
long ago when it could all have been very different. Barely
three years before the establishment of the State the surviving Jews of the world were wondering and asking themselves whether there was in fact any future for the Jewish
people at all — whether this people could muster the
energy, the tenacity and the courage required in order to
overcome the catastrophe that had just befallen it. It was
not so long ago when the remnants of Jewish communities
not very far from here were asking themselves whether
there was any reason or hope for continuing. Some put this
question to a vote! Those that survived — and there were
very few — asked themselves whether there was any reason, justification or sense in rebuilding the ruins and
almost came to the point of saying: those of us who have
survived will now quietly walk off the stage and into that
oblivion into which disappeared the rest and the best of us.
But they and all of us decided differently and embarked
upon that triumphant Jewish riposte to what had been
perpetrated against the Jewish people. That is what the

State of Israel is — the emphatic answer and bold riposte of the Jewish people to what was done to it and the only guarantee against its repetition.

We have fought five wars since we came into being. Security continues to be our most important single undertaking. Without security there is nothing. That is the linchpin, the basis and the infrastructure upon which the entire edifice is built. The business of security is Israel's exclusive business. Unlike any other country we alone are responsible for our security and wish nobody else ever to share the responsibility with us. There is not a single European country that is responsible for its own security. European security today is a joint American-European venture. We are the only country in the world that *insists* on being able to defend itself by itself. Why? Because we know better. Because we know we are the only ones capable of responding with the swiftness, efficiency and determination required to prevent disaster. In matters of security we trust no one and can entrust nothing to anyone. The next few years will therefore continue to involve the greatest possible effort in order to further ensure that Israel's vital and enormous security needs are adequately met. The costs are staggering. Very few countries, if any, can afford to carry such a defence burden as ours. There is no other country that allocates 30% of its national budget annually to defence as we do. And we do this by ourselves. It is not within the power and the capacity and ability of all of World Jewry to help measurably in shouldering this burden. Security is our business — exclusively. In order to be able to discharge this business and duty, we have mortgaged ourselves unto generations to come. Hence if you wish, some of the answers to some of the questions that may be intriguing you in connection with Israel's economic problems. Such things as three-digit inflation figures are a function of the business of shouldering the defence of Israel alone. That is our business and so it will remain.

But that is not all we do. Israel is not a Sparta and neither is it an Athens. *Israel is Jerusalem.* We have not set up shop in the Middle East to become one more little country among many. We are not just one of over a hundred and fifty members of the United Nations. We are a Jewish State — *the only Jewish State.* And this involves special responsibility. The country that we have established for the Jewish people in the ancient Jewish homeland is not meant to be a run-of-the-mill country but a country of excellence. Excellence, because that is the tradition we must uphold. Excellence, because unless we excel we shall not be able to fulfil our mission. The future of Israel depends on its ability to continue to do better than most if not all. That is also how we mean to compensate for the deficiency in numbers. We are few, very few, and until masses of Jews come — when and if they come — we will continue to be few. To redress this imbalance in numbers we must have quality and excellence.

This is easier said than done. Maintaining the standard of excellence that we expect of ourselves — that *you* expect of us — involves a massive job of national rebuilding. For what is Israel? It is a collective of everything that is Jewish. Not only of the Jewish communities of the entire world — of those that no longer exist and those that continue to exist — but also of *everything Jewish.* Where everything and everyone have come together — where East and West have met after two millennia of separate parallel existence.

53

We are the home to which oppressed Jews have come in search of a refuge. We are the place to which remnants of persecuted communities have fled. With them they brought the bag and baggage of their diverse experiences across many centuries. All this has come and collected in Israel. All this is yet to be welded and meshed, all this is yet to be fully blended into a harmonious whole. This is not an undertaking that can be expected to be completed in thirty-four years. When you hear therefore of problems and tensions, of difficulties and of polemics, it is the process of coming-togetherness that you are hearing. It is the clash and the friction of the diverse communities which make up the Jewish people of Israel, all coming together. It is a search for harmony that you are hearing. Not a harmony in which all of these unique cultural experiences and attributes will become lost in one monolithic whole in which we will all look the same, act the same, talk the same, think the same. That would not be in the nature of Jewishness as a constant *individual* search for comprehension and for learning, for betterment and for accomplishment. We are a people of enormous talent and just as equally also a very diverse people. That diversity must be maintained.

As we make our way through all this we also have to make a living. Israel is a poor country bereft of everything that others take for granted. And yet, in those thirty-four years that we have been talking about, Israel has become a very substantial economic enterprise. A country which today exports over ten billion dollars worth of goods annually. A country that today produces everything from avocados to supersonic planes and all of the highest quality. Ladies and gentlemen, there may be misgivings about

54

certain things and there must not be the slightest doubt whatsoever: the Israel that we are here to serve is a success story without parallel. No other people has been able to raise itself from the ashes and proceed to create as remarkable and as brilliant a society as that which we have — against all odds — wrought and fashioned.

This is the premise from which you should proceed and no other. This Israel is not a poor relative. Not a little fly-by-night country. Not a needy country. We may have needs but we are not needy. That support which you give us, is important — very important. *But* all the support which World Jewry gives the State of Israel in one year amounts to 4% of the national budget of Israel. No more. At the same time the support you give us is immensely important for two main reasons: it is important for those very projects and causes in whose aid the money is raised and these invariably involve *all-Jewish* needs and not exclusive "Israeli" needs for they are all in one way or another connected with the ongoing process of ingathering and reconstruction. The other reason why we continue to come out and address JIA dinners and do so with the fullest conviction that this is critically important and that it must not merely be continued but that every effort be made to redouble it, is that this provides you with an indispensable instrumentality for being associated with us, for being involved in our efforts, for being identified with our struggle, not only in word but in deed. This is not only important for you. It is important for us. We need to know that this enterprise for which we have assumed the responsibility is a joint enterprise. An *all-Jewish* enterprise. After all, you could very easily have been there and we here. If a ship had sailed in another direction or if a grandfather had decided to go elsewhere, one of you people would be standing up here tonight and I would be sitting down there. It is critically important that Israelis continue to be assured of what they deeply believe to be true, namely that they are part of a larger whole, that theirs is not a private adventure, that they are discharging their duties not just on behalf of their immediate selves but on behalf of the entire Jewish people. It makes an enormous difference. It gives us and the whole struggle and enterprise a special meaning — if you wish a special dimension. It is therefore important that never, never, never, will Israelis have reason to suspect, fear or suddenly conclude that they have been left holding the bag. That would be the greatest shock, the greatest trauma of all. That must never happen. Thus the JIA, the "University Friends" the institutes and the institutions — everything that provides Jews in the Diaspora with opportunities to associate themselves with this enterprise which we Israelis continue to look upon not as our exclusive preserve but as belonging to all of us. We are in this boat together and it is a sturdy boat, a fine boat, and a swift boat and it is a boat that will with God's help — and with everyone's help — reach safe haven in our times.

On "Article 51" and
the Right to Self-Defence and
on Allegations Concerning
Israeli Arms Supplies

London, May 17, 1982

For Israel, defence continues to be a massive and exacting undertaking. The completion of its withdrawal from Sinai deprived Israel of what for almost a decade and a half was one of its most important security assets — the wide expanses of desert and the elaborate infrastructure established there. We hope, indeed we pray, that the peace for the sake of which we gave up this critical buffer will prove to be sufficient and lasting recompense. Along the rest of the Arab-Israeli line not only does peace continue to elude us but the threats and the dangers have not abated. This is true especially in the north, where an entity committed to the elimination of the state and the people of Israel has established itself with an increasingly substantial military capacity, threatening lives and property along Israel's northern borders.

Last week, after yet another series of terrorist attacks, Israel, exercising as much right to self-defence as anyone else, took action against terrorist bases in southern Lebanon from which these and other attacks against it — as well as most acts of international terrorism — have been

57

repeatedly launched. While we can never be sure of the military results of the actions we may be obliged to take, we are hardly ever in any doubt as to some of the flak which almost invariably attends them. Nevertheless, we were somewhat surprised by the intensity of the condemnation in this country of our recent air actions along the Lebanese border. To the best of my knowledge the British statement was the sharpest made by any EEC country.

It is not the intention or practice of Israel to pass judgement on other people's conflicts and actions. At the same time it is suggested that those who seek recourse in Article 51 of the UN Charter in support of military action taken in self-defence, should recall that like the rest of the UN Charter, Article 51 was not meant to be invoked or put into practice selectively. What is good enough in the protection of national interests should be good enough in the protection of national survival.

To paraphrase *The Times* of this morning: *Israelis too have rights*! And these include — not as *The Times* suggests — a claim to "total security" but to basic physical security, for state and people alike.

There has been no more flagrant violation of the UN Charter than denying Israel this most elementary of rights by all those member-states of the United Nations who, as they cynically cajole others to support their outlandish resolutions against Israel — which *The Times* of this morning would have us heed — openly proclaim their right to unremitting war against it. When did *The Times* or anyone else for that matter last denounce *this* aggression? Aggression continuously committed against Israel over thirty-four years is no less noteworthy than one which is claimed to be in effect for some forty days against others.

58

Much as we have tried to keep a discreet distance from the South Atlantic crisis we have not been allowed to be exempted from it. As you may have noticed the media have repeatedly made critical references to alleged Israeli arms sales. Our efforts to refute these allegations, which I wish to emphasize once again are completely without foundation, have been less than successful. The insinuations stubbornly persist. Indeed, even when a weapon used in this conflict was very clearly not of Israeli manufacture it was suggested that at the very least the training of the party using the weapon was Israel's responsibility. On May 9, the *Sunday Times* in an "Insight" report on the lethal qualities of a non-Israeli missile by the name of "Exocet" had this to say: "If the Argentinians were not trained by the French before the conflict started who taught them? There are several countries with the knowhow but the most likely is Israel..."

Within two days a sister-paper of the *Sunday Times* refuted this allegation. Quoting an "authoritative source", *The Times* of May 11 said: "...they (the Argentines) are no fools; they did it themselves"...

The trouble is that while the first report which cited Israel specifically was printed on the front page of the *Sunday Times,* the second report which amounted to a dismissal of these allegations appeared in an inside page of *The Times* — where it may well belong. As a result, the impression that must continue to linger in the public mind is the incriminating one created by the front-page story in the *Sunday Times.*

This episode and others like it, raise some questions:

Why when mentioning "several countries" with a knowledge of the use of the "Exocet" missile was Israel the

59

only one cited by name *and* especially when there was not the slightest factual basis for this assertion?

Why when enumerating and assessing the various arms and weapon systems in the Argentinian arsenal are those of Israeli manufacture or origin invariably quoted as such while other weapons in use by the Argentinian armed forces — far more numerous and deadly — originating in other countries, including Britain, are referred to as if they had some lunar source?

How does one account for the manner in which the same prominence is given — in a recent question raised in an important debate — to the earth-shaking issue of whether or not Israel "is supplying ammunition to the Argentinians" as to such matters as an expression of admiration for the forces which recaptured South Georgia; the need for more information on the situation and the importance of all-party discussion? A reference to alleged Israeli ammunition supplies alongside such a distinguished string of queries would be just as odd even if it had any basis in fact — which it does not.

Why — to repeat an old and battered refrain — *"why pick on us"*? Why pick on us when we could easily argue — which we continue to restrain ourselves from doing — that in matters relating to arms supplies it is we who have so much cause for grievance. It is after all Israel which — since 1973 — has been the victim of an arms embargo while some of Israel's adversaries have been on the receiving end of some of the most sophisticated and lethal weapons produced.

Above all, why pick on us when there is no reason known to us for casting such aspersions on our conduct? For the record's sake let me repeat yet again what we have said time and again: Since the beginning of the South Atlantic crisis Israel has been scrupulous in avoiding any involvement in it. This includes specifically the matter of arms supplies. All allegations and insinuations to the contrary are totally without foundation.

In saying this we do not wish or need to apologise for anything. We do so only for the record's sake and in perhaps the vain hope of setting it straight now that it has been so unfairly and unjustly falsified. In the final analysis we do this in the defence of Israel against, among so many other things, the threat of defamation.

2

Israel
and the Jewish People

What's Wrong with Israel?

Jews' College, London, June 30, 1980

Distinguished and much esteemed Chief Rabbi Dr. Jakobovits and Mrs. Jakobovits, Lady Brodie, distinguished officers of the College, ladies and gentlemen, I am truly honoured to be invited to address you here at Jews' College, a great centre of Jewish scholarship and Jewish education.

I was brought up to recognise Jewish education as the most important and effective instrument for ensuring the continued survival and unity of the Jewish people. When asked what he considered the most effective means for preserving the Diaspora's link with Israel, Ben-Gurion always answered: "חינוך עברי :עברית" — "Hebrew: Jewish Education!". And this is true today even more than in his days.

I am sorry to hear about the deficit. I can only say you are in excellent company — if that is any comfort — but I am sure that given the commitment of this community to the values and ideals of Jewish education these problems will soon be effectively overcome.

Ladies and gentlemen, these are difficult times, perhaps among the most difficult we have ever experienced. It is important, therefore, that we discuss the issues of these times as honestly and as candidly as we can. The Jewish agenda is full and it includes some extremely critical items. In a sense the sum total of the agenda is the very future of

65

our people. It is therefore no wonder that the debate over this agenda is as intense as it is and it is fitting that Israel should be at the centre of it.

Recently the distinguished leader of a distinguished Jewish organization — Mr. Edgar Bronfman of the World Jewish Congress — made a statement in which he listed a host of deficiencies which he diagnosed in present-day Israel and which added up to a very disturbing picture. I suggest that we take up that picture as presented by Mr. Bronfman and adopt that list of defects and deficiencies which he detected in Israel as the agenda for our discussion here this evening and in this manner seek to arrive at an understanding of what does or does not afflict Israel today so that we may either prescribe the remedies required or else reassure ourselves that things are perhaps not half as bad as is being suggested.

Here is what Mr. Bronfman had to say in a column written for the WJC publication *News and Views* of February-March 1980:

The Jewish world is facing difficult times.

Israel, which is central to the Jewish people, is despite its unique accomplishments, having very serious trouble.

At least as many people are leaving that country as are going. We do not precisely know why some 500,000 Israelis have left. Or why for some time now only 30% of those who have been allowed to leave Russia choose to go to Israel (nor do we know how many of the 30% stay in Israel once they get there).... Israel has rampant inflation, abysmal productivity and social services it cannot afford. Dissension exists over the handling of

66

the West Bank and its one million plus Arabs.... Israel also has dismally failed to deal adequately with its Sephardi population, some 60% of the Jews in Israel.... There is growing anxiety over a country splintered by a proportional representative system that doesn't work now, and, in its thirty-one-year history, never really has.... There is disappointment in a country which is less than what the original Zionists envisioned — an Israel which we wanted to think of as the embodiment of Jewish ideals: fairness, justice, wisdom.... It is an Israel which, largely because of its political system, has been unable to become the repository of the Jewish ideal; a country which expects its fellow Jews living abroad, especially in the United States, to "hold the line" for it, no matter what.... It is a country which, by reason of the much more fecund rate of births by the Sephardi and Arab populations than by the Ashkenazi, will become increasingly a Middle Eastern country, and thus much less a place where the average Western (or even Soviet) Jew will feel at home.

Thus is Israel depicted by a gentleman who presides over an organization that is not unimportant. With your permission, may I now take up every point on Mr. Bronfman's list of woes and attempt to see whether the indictment is accurate or justified.

The first complaint listed by Mr. Bronfman is the scourge of inflation. Truly a critical area of concern, for inflation is not only a monetary problem. It is a condition which can gnaw away at the very foundations of a state and a society. We plead guilty to the charge: Israel's inflation is truly of alarming proportions. But how come there

67

is this inflation? What does it consist of? Israel's budget is divided into roughly three parts: almost 30% is committed for defence. Another 30% is earmarked for the servicing of debts incurred in years past, again mostly for defence requirements. What is left is slated for the financing of all those services that a modern society like Israel requires. Is it any wonder that in 1979 inflation in Israel reached 111%?! The next question we should ask ourselves is whether all the money invested in defence has yielded a profitable return. I submit to you that it has. When in the annals of history has a little country as poor and as outnumbered as Israel, given a better account of itself in this, the most critical area of the testing of nations and in Israel's case involving a conflict of no less than thirty-two years' duration? Have these years of supreme national investment provided a profitable return? I submit to you that the answer is yes! We have *won* the war! We have made *peace.* It has not been a war without end. It is a war whose end we have begun to witness. Peace — that is what we have begun to realise on our enormous investment in war. If today we have to bear the economic consequences of this unique achievement, then surely these are dwarfed by the magnitude of the achievement.

Mr. Bronfman complains about Israel's poor — "abysmal" productivity. There are many people here tonight who do business with Israel and whom I frequently encounter at meetings of the Anglo-Israel Chamber of Commerce and elsewhere where important matters relating to the economic development of Israel are being promoted and advanced by this community. These gentlemen will no doubt readily attest to Israel's economic achievements. This "unproductive" little country of Israel is

68

today exporting annually eight billion dollars worth of goods — a substantial part of which are *industrial* products! There are five countries in the world that produce medical scanners, only five. Israel is one of those five. There are at the most five or six countries in the world that produce supersonic aircraft. Israel is one of those five. There are few countries that can boast of an industry and technology and a scientific base like Israel's. And the proof is in this tremendous achievement which is represented by that figure of eight billion dollars of exports last year alone. And this is the same little country which has so much to cope with and which has nonetheless produced the effort, the skills and the resources that account for eight billion dollars' worth of exports. Business is not philanthropy: nobody does anything for nothing and nobody does anybody any favours. We would not do this volume of business unless we were productive. We would not be able to sell unless we were competitive. So we must be somewhat more productive than Mr. Bronfman suggests.

Mr. Bronfman complains about the social services which we provide and which he says we cannot afford. Perhaps we cannot afford them in purely financial terms. But there are other criteria for judging Israel's allegedly exorbitantly costly social services and the alleged failure to absorb that vast number of people who came to us from Arabic-speaking countries in the Middle East and North Africa.

What are the social services for if not to establish a base on which we can build the structure that will bridge the gap between these underprivileged immigrants and the rest of the society, that will tide these people over until they are

69

able to raise themselves up to the levels and standards of the rest of the community? What are these services for if not that? And if they are beyond the means and capacity of little Israel to provide, then all the more reason why Israel deserves every commendation for having expended so much of its resources in order to enable its less fortunate citizens to start at least from a higher base. And that base is none other than the network of social services that we provide and which may indeed be beyond our means.

Mr. Bronfman complains about proportional representation as being the scourge of Israeli politics. Ladies and gentlemen, one of the most glorious achievements of Israel is that in thirty-two years of constant warfare which anywhere else would have led to at least one military takeover, the country continues to function as a perfect parliamentary democracy. Israel continues to be a country in which the people decide through their representatives as elected by them in accordance with a system that has been in operation now for thirty-two years and which has provided leadership for Israel throughout as many years with, I think, remarkable results. It is also a system that is particularly well suited to the temperaments and idiosyncrasies of the Jewish people and which caters to literally every Jewish whim and passion. All facets of the political spectrum find expression in Israel, from one extreme to the other, and we have all the extremes. We have no cause for anything but pride in our parliamentary democracy — cumbersome, voluble and even shrill as it may sometimes seem.

Another very serious charge levelled at us by Mr. Bronfman is that the Jewish state has not lived up to his expectations. Let us consider this charge. Everywhere in the world and most especially in the country where Mr. Bronfman presently resides the one greatest single danger facing the Jewish people is *disappearance*. Disappearance is the consequence of the lack of Jewish values and Jewish commitments of the kind that have sustained us through the ages. As for Israel what is it if not the truly ultimate attempt of the Jewish people *not* to disappear? That is what Israel is — the Jewish people's commitment to the ultimate Jewish commitment, namely survival. Let no one cast aspersions on that.

Then there is the charge that Israel is becoming an increasingly Levantine state — which would appear to be in conflict with the complaint about shortcomings in the absorption of immigrants from Arabic-speaking countries. I don't know what Israel is going to become. I think it is too early to tell but I suspect that ultimately it is going to be the synthesis of all of the strains of Jewish life and culture. I can't think of a more appropriate, or more historically just result than that Israel should become the synthesis of all the Jewish strains of the Jewish world. And if it becomes somewhat less European in complexion and if it becomes somewhat more Middle Eastern in complexion, so be it. The Middle East is the font of our history. That is where we came from. And if we are destined to look and sound more like our forefathers today then I, for one, say by all means!

I have tried to defend Israel. But I also concede its blemishes and defects and weaknesses. Yes, we *are* tired, we *are* exhausted, we *are* impoverished by thirty-two years of non-stop war. We have expended all our material resources. But that is not the real price, the only price and the most costly price we have paid. Mr. Bronfman cites the

71

decline of certain standards and of certain norms. Ladies and gentlemen, we miss in Israel today thousands of the most beautiful young people that could ever have been — the future professors and the directors and the teachers and the rabbis that have died in the wars of Israel. That is what we miss in Israel today. That is our most painful defect. A piece has been torn out of us, the most precious one. The finest that Israel produces are also the first to go. When in 1973 we lost over 3,000 soldiers, 50% were officers and NCO's who would have gone on to become the most beautiful Israelis and who are no longer there. That is the price we have paid and to the consequences of that price we plead guilty.

We sound, we appear, we act in a somewhat disorderly fashion these days. But then what is Israel? Who are we Israelis? I will tell you who we are. In addition to representing the finest in the Jewish world we are also a collection of all of the miseries of the Jewish world. That's what we are. Who comes to Israel today? Who flees to Israel? The poor, the underprivileged, the persecuted. Those who have nowhere else to go. And they come shorn and lacking many of those attributes which in this country and elsewhere in Europe one usually expects of a Jew. Education? lacking! Upbringing? lacking! Manners? lacking! Poverty? galore! That is what Israel is. Sixty percent of our population is of underprivileged origin. We took them all. That is what we exist for. Is it any wonder that there are defects and blemishes? What have we taken in if not *all* of the defects and *all* of the blemishes of two thousand years of exile, deprivation, persecution and humiliation as practised in the extreme against the Jews of Arab lands in particular.

72

For all this we are today being castigated. Not only by Mr. Bronfman, and he will forgive me for using him as an illustration. He is not the only one who is presently complaining and bemoaning the state of the republic and the people of Israel. Such seems to be the view of many others, *including* Israelis.

Let me now say a few words about the corollary of that view, namely the view *from* Israel. The view which Israelis are increasingly beginning to have of the Jews abroad, of the Jewish world outside Israel. Just as it is important for us to discuss honestly, candidly and responsibly what you find wrong with us in Israel, so I think it is important, perhaps more important, that you know that there is growing concern in Israel today, about the Jewish world in the Diaspora. It may be unjustified but it is a fact that I think must be addressed, and the sooner the better. For there is concern in Israel as well as disappointment and disillusionment.

Mr. Bronfman spoke about the rights of people in his position who make monetary contributions to Israel to express an opinion about anything and everything. Monetary contributions are not necessarily the best credentials for passing judgement on Israel, for we accept criticism from every Jew whether from the heights of the Seagram Building or anywhere else. As for monetary contributions to Israeli causes let me say this: Ladies and gentlemen, what Israel receives today from the Jewish world is a pittance and whatever there is of it is hardly earmarked for Israel proper. Certainly not for me and not for my children. This money serves only one purpose today: to enable us to take care of those "olim" who come to Israel today — and some *do* come — because we really have no other

73

resources on which to draw in order to provide for the needs of new immigrants given our present economic difficulties and the immense burdens which we carry today. All the rest is our business. Let me give you an idea of the economic burden that we carry and nobody else carries except us. Recently we signed a peace agreement with Egypt which inter alia called for the evacuation of airfields in Sinai and the construction of other airfields in the Negev. The United States government was kind enough to extend to us a loan for that purpose — a *loan* not a grant. The annual servicing of that loan alone is the equivalent of the entire annual proceeds of the UJA in the US! That is how much we carry and let me hasten to say that money which the UJA raises is not earmarked for anything except immigrant absorption. The money raised for the building of airfields and the construction of the defence infrastructure that we have now had to transplant from Sinai to the south of Israel, and all the ongoing normal enormous defence burden that we have to carry is going to be paid for by no less than perhaps three generations of Israelis to come! That is how mortgaged we are. That is the extent of our foreign debt. That is the extent of our financial obligation for defence and this is the sort of money that has not been raised in all of the years of fund-raising campaigns put together. That is what *we* Israelis have invested — financially — in the state of the Jewish people.

Now I come to the most painful complaint that we Israelis have. We don't really complain very much about the manner or the degree to which people extend to us financial assistance these days. We are gradually getting used to our disproportionate share. There is one thing however that really breaks our hearts. Hardly anybody comes. Other than classic hardship aliya very few Jews come to Israel today. Immigration, as Mr. Bronfman says, is almost down to a tiny trickle and one asks oneself whether it is historically justified that only that small band of Jews that make up the people of Israel in Israel should alone shoulder the responsibility of manning the battlements of the Land of Israel. Three million Jews in all. That is all there is of us in Israel. Three million in thirty-two years. That is all the Jews who have come to Israel or have been born in Israel. The majority of the Jewish people live elsewhere. You might say that times are bad and not conducive to immigration to Israel. Was there a better time than the immediate post-1967 era when all the dreams seemed to have been fulfilled? When Israel was also the darling of the world? Certainly the darling of the Jewish people. How many came then? The only ones who came then and who come today are those who come to Israel because their commitment to Judaism is complete and who come to live a Jewish life in Israel. Yes, religious Jews come to Israel. Very few others come. And those who come bring along with them also some of the passions that have led them there and which ultimately also find a way into the political debate in Israel, which is perfectly legitimate. The absence of reinforcements is the most painful of our disappointments. We have, it seems, been left to fend for ourselves. And then there is another thing that is developing into a source of disillusionment and also of concern — namely, the declining solidarity with Israel at a time when we need it most, at a time when we have to make some literally existential decisions and at a time when we find ourselves at the receiving end of increasingly escalating and heavier international pressure. The most recent

75

example of this was the statement issued by the European Economic Community in Venice. If the Community's prescription for so-called peace in the Middle East is ever to be implemented it will be tantamount to the demise of the State of Israel. Moreover, the Community is not just stating its position. It is also engaged for the first time in a diplomatic effort towards the implementation of its programme. And there are hints of a diplomatic effort that will also be backed up by pressure.

We need today all the support we can get in order to be able to contend with what I think may well develop into considerable pressure on Israel to accept formulas that it simply cannot possibly accept, not because of caprice, but because we know from experience, that we simply cannot ensure the continued security, prosperity and very survival of Israel in such conditions as are being put forward.

I wish to submit to you that we are perhaps at a juncture which is more critical than we may suspect, when the Jews of the State of Israel are beginning to wonder whether they have not been left holding the bag. The Jews of the State of Israel are beginning to ask themselves whether they have been left to fend for themselves. This may be unjustified — certainly when I look at the people present here tonight and after hearing what the Chief Rabbi had to say about the centrality of Israel — and yet there is doubt, there is concern and anxiety.

This has hardly been lost on the onlookers. In the Councils of the Nine one notices today — when the problems of the Middle East are being discussed — an attempt to make a distinction between the Jews and the State of Israel. This is not surprising, for it makes it easier to pursue certain policies once they are not directed at the Jewish people —

which would involve a deep, moral dilemma — certainly in Europe. Such policies are much easier to practice once Israel is less than synonymous with the Jewish people. And this becomes possible and feasible once cracks are discerned in the Jewish ranks. They too hear the dissension and they too see that potential olim choose to go elsewhere. And they too know that Israel is plagued with enormous problems which with all the alleged might of the Jewish people have proven very difficult to surmount. We seem to have arrived at a point when Israelis are deeply concerned about flagging Jewish commitment and when onlookers are beginning to wonder about them too. I need not elaborate on the dangers that such doubts pose for all of us. I do wish only to comment on one especially poignant aspect of this state of affairs. When we started out in 1948 we thought we were a different brand of Jews. We looked down on the Diaspora. We were a break with the past. We were the "New Jews". Today, thirty-two years later, there is no more Jewish-minded and committed community of Jews in the world than the State of Israel. There is nowhere more "Ahavat Israel" and the sense of Jewish belongingness; a sense of Jewish commonality and a commitment to Judaism — to the faith and the glory and the future of the Jewish people — than those which you find in Israel today. Thirty-two years later we Israelis have become more Jewish than the Jews. Thirty-two years later we are totally identified with the Jewish people and thirty-two years later it is *we* who are wondering whether the Jews are keeping a distance from *us*. I would be remiss if I did not tell you that this is what one hears and what one senses today. There is a growing suspicion in Israel that we have been left holding not only the bag but also the banner

77

— the Jewish banner. This dangerous state of affairs or mind is perhaps the most important single item on that agenda which I referred to when I opened my remarks by saying "the agenda is full". How we Jews deal with this item is really not up to us in Israel. We have our hands full. Moreover the circle is now complete. We have become the most Jewish of the Jews and it is now up to the rest to live up to their commitment as Jews. Thank you very much.

A Tribute to Dutch Courage

Speech on the Occasion of
the Presentation of the Yad Vashem Awards at
the Koninklijk Instituut voor de Tropen
Amsterdam, September 11, 1978

Once again we have come together to pay homage to a band of Dutch men and women who not so very long ago dared at great peril to themselves and their families to cling to their humanity and decency while the world around them was sinking into unprecedented barbarism. Once again we are assembled in order to express to them and to all those others represented by them the gratitude and admiration of the Jewish people for saving the lives of desperate Jewish men, women and children from that fate which was reserved for them under the terms of what was to have been "The Final Solution of the Jewish problem".

Some were saved. The overwhelming majority were not. Nazi Germany failed to realise its diabolical grand scheme. It did succeed however in achieving one of its prime objectives, namely the destruction of most of the Jews of Continental Europe. In contrast with Nazi Germany the Allied powers took little interest in the fate of the Jews of Europe. Although they were *known* to be a prime and central target of Nazi bestiality and although the details of their destruction were *known* at an early stage, the saving of the Jews of Europe was never an acknowledged or even implicit war aim of the Allies. At no time during the Second World War was there any concerted, emphatic and resolute attempt to try and stop the systematic extermination that was *known* to be in full swing all over Europe. At no time was there any real effort to try and effectively *deter* the Nazis from embarking upon their infernal scheme. On the contrary ample cause was given them to conclude that the world would remain silent. Such was for example the net effect of the abortive conference of the so-called Nations of Asylum which assembled in Evian-les-Bains in July 1938 — fifteen weeks after Hitler annexed Austria — in order to consider ways and means of saving his prospective victims there and in Germany.

When at the end of a long and heated session it was time for the countries present to make their concrete commitments, the delegates rose one by one to offer their excuses for doing absolutely nothing. Only three countries showed any real willingness to help; these were: Holland, Denmark and The Dominican Republic. But their goodwill came to nothing once the Conference officially resolved to limit its scope only to Jewish refugees who could pay their way, knowing full well that no Jew could leave Germany or Austria with more than five Reichsmark. Four months later, on November 9, 1938, came the Kristallnacht. By the end of that month "Das Schwarze Korps", the official newspaper of the SS, could flagrantly write: "Because it is necessary, because we no longer hear the world's screeching and because, after all, no power on earth can hinder us, we will now bring the Jewish question to its total solution."

The more is revealed of the history of that period the more damning is the evidence. A recent study by Martin Gilbert, the prominent British historian, reveals still further harrowing facts, such as the episode only six months before the war when Britain and the US asked Nazi Germany to discourage Jewish travel in ships bound for Palestine and "to check unauthorized emigration of Jews from the Reich". *After* the war began Britain refused to permit 20,000 Jewish children to go to Palestine from Poland on the grounds that to do so would free the Germans from the economic burden of having to feed them, thus helping the Nazi war effort. And a secret Foreign Office document expressed the hope that all German Jews would be "stuck at the mouth of the Danube for lack of ships to take them".

There may have been a lack of ships but there was no shortage of trains. Indeed the transport of Jews to their death often had priority over the German war effort itself. While everything else collapsed and crumbled, the business of exterminating Jews continued unabated until literally the last days of the war. While the saving of Jewish lives figured very low, if at all, on the list of Allied war aims, the liquidation of European Jewry was at the very top of Nazi Germany's list. The inevitable result of this terrible asymmetry was the greatest catastrophe that ever befell the Jewish people.

We repeat these harrowing facts today more with pain and sadness than with bitterness or rancour. Time has taken its toll of our emotions too. We repeat them however as no mere elucidation of a chapter of our past that is unparalleled either in the annals of ours or any other people. We repeat them as a critical point of reference in the charting of our future. And we do so with special emphasis on this day. For as we are assembled here today, a historic conference is taking place in Camp David near

81

Washington where the leaders of Egypt and Israel have come together at the invitation of the President of the United State in order to seek — and hopefully to find — ways and means of resolving the conflict between them. While it may perhaps be excessive and unrealistic to expect this conference to produce a magic formula that will immediately usher in a new era of Arab-Israeli relations, there is little doubt that Camp David is a historic milestone in the quest for such an era.

This is not the place nor the occasion to discuss the details of Israel's positions and proposals in Camp David or elsewhere. But it is very much the place and the occasion to state most authoritatively that those are moulded and stamped at least as much by the lessons of the past as by the circumstances of the present. Not only by Prime Minister Begin whose soul is scorched by his European experience which included the destruction of his entire family. It is also shaped by every other member of the Israeli delegation — practically all of them products of the soil and the sun of the Land of Israel. All of them share one fundamental and immutable point of departure and reference — the unique national experience of the Jewish people as climaxed by the Holocaust. This experience taught one lesson: Never must we forget what was done to the Jewish people. Never must we trust *anyone* to guarantee and protect us against yet another attempt on the life of the Jewish people. Little or nothing that has happened to the Jewish people since the establishment of its third sovereign Commonwealth in the Land of our Fathers casts any doubt on this conviction.

In the final analysis we have been as lonely since achieving statehood as we were before. And may I be permitted to say candidly to you today that to the many traumas of our people has lately been added yet another one and by that I refer to the manner in which for months on end now the Government and people of Israel have been subjected to a vicious smear campaign that makes those of us who have never experienced a full-fledged pogrom understand better what it must have been like. To those who have participated in this pogrom: those who pass resolutions labelling us racists; those who then adopt such terminology in their campaign of slander against us; those who compare our leaders with the monsters of Nazi Germany; those who openly preach the replacement of Israel by a non-Zionist entity and who do so under the emblem of an assassin brandishing a Soviet Kalachnikov machine gun of the kind that was used in the killing of Israeli school children, athletes and passengers on a bus; those who advocate the public subvention of the activities of these people; those who publicly argue that the killing of an Israeli Jew is more permissible than that of another Jew; those who rally to the defence of such a doctrine; those who write about the day when the Amalekites and the Philistines of old will finally take their revenge; those who say they are not anti-Jewish but only anti-Zionist. To all those we say: Every libellous thing you have said about us, every slanderous word you have written about us, all the scorn and abuse you have heaped on us have strengthened us in our resolve never to flinch and never to be deterred, never to forget and also never to put our trust in anyone but ourselves. That has been your only achievement and for this we are indebted to you: for having reminded us yet again of the reality with which we as Jews must always contend and against which we must always brace ourselves.

And no one is better qualified to understand and sympathize with this age-old anguish of the Jewish people than the people whom we honour here today for they were witnesses once before to the magnitude of Jewish despair. To them I wish to say: You have been witnesses to our greatest tragedy but you have also seen our greatest triumph: the re-establishment of sovereign Jewish statehood and nationhood in the land of Israel. This has really been your greatest reward. Since then you have followed our trials and tribulations and on more than one occasion you must have looked on with horror as our renewed and rejuvenated people appeared threatened and sometimes doomed. Every time this happened you were rewarded yet again by witnessing the salvation of Israel yet another time. Your greatest and most bountiful reward is however yet to come and it will come. The day is not far off when Israel will live in peace with its neighbours — a generous peace and a secure peace. That I know will be the keenest gratification we can offer you for having stood by our people in their hour of greatest need. For this we thank you and this good and decent land of yours.

Greetings on the
Eve of the High Holidays

London, September 1980

The year 5741 promises to be a year of decisions and the decisions may well be critical to the future of Israel and the Jewish people.

The coming year will be a year of confluence — the confluence of all the processes and pressures that have been building up for many months now and which threaten to converge at a certain moment within the framework of 5741 and to combine into a massive attempt to force upon Israel a formula for a purported resolution of the Arab-Israeli dispute which Israel has already concluded it cannot and will not accept. Not because of caprice or idiosyncrasy but because what is contemplated runs counter to the national consensus on what Israel can live with and what it cannot live without.

There is little that is not already known about the formula that is envisaged. We have had ample advance notice of it in the form of an avalanche of statements and proclamations ranging from the Venice Declaration of the European Economic Community to innumerable United Nations resolutions. What is contemplated is Israel's return to insecure lines of defence. What is advocated is the abandonment of Israeli control over areas critical to its minimum security. What is increasingly called for is the

85

creation of an entity sworn to the very undoing of the State of Israel and what is proclaimed is a call for the division of Jerusalem. All this runs against the very grain of a wide and solid Israeli consensus arrived at in the exercise of the inalienable and elementary right of the people of Israel to national and physical survival.

We have no cause for complaint about the fact that this is the intention of that unholy alliance of enemies and detractors of the State of Israel. They at least lay no claim to wish Israel well. We do, however, have grounds to protest and deplore the fact that such notions and designs should be increasingly endorsed and supported by those who insist on their right to be looked upon as Israel's friends. Far be it from Israel to question or reject professions of friendship towards itself and its people. And yet, we cannot but take note of the manner in which the demands upon Israel are becoming increasingly related to the growing deference on the part of many who claim to be our friends to the dictates of those who today hold to ransom proud and noble nations; whose whims determine which countries shall prosper and which shall not; whose actions have the effect of deciding how many millions shall go without employment; whose policies threaten to plunge vast numbers of people into economic and political chaos; whose greed has sealed the fate of poor emerging nations and who seek above all to exercise their vast economic prowess in order to strangle the Jewish state of Israel.

Recently we have all been shocked witnesses to a sample of what is contemplated and the manner in which it is to be brought about when Israel's resolve to resist any attempt to wrest its eternal capital from it became the pretext for the application of massive blackmail on friendly countries in order to force them to take geographical and political distance from Jerusalem. It was not Israel which sought this test. Rather it was forced upon it by all those who elected to yield to pressure and blackmail and in so doing lent their sponsorship to the elevation of the issue of Jerusalem to the top of the political agenda instead of heeding Israel's counselling that no one discount or belittle its commitment to the very fount of its history. In cavalierly ignoring Israel's determined commitment to its eternal capital a blow has been dealt to a difficult and complex search for peace — a just and equitable peace which was also to include a magnanimous and generous provision for the sensitivities and devotions of all who hold Jerusalem dear. That is the manner in which nations have been cajoled into frantic submissive action by those who have nothing but disdain not only for Israel and its cherished capital but also for the welfare of the entire civilised world.

No more eloquent or macabre demonstration of the growing submissiveness on the part of this same civilised world is the manner in which it is making available the genius of its industrial technology in order to provide the enemies of Israel with vast quantities of ever more sophisticated arms with which Israel is to be brought to its knees as was recently on public display in this country at an international aeronautical exhibition of the most frightful assortment of lethal weapons freely available to anyone who can afford to buy them with little regard for their intended victims.

Such are the circumstances and conditions in which Israel may well be put to the test of decision-making in this coming year. Such are the odds which Israel will have to contend with and such is the magnitude of the decision which Israel will be called upon to make. And yet there is confidence in our hearts as we approach this coming year of decision. The enmity is *not* total. There is peace between Israel and its former leading adversary. The might of those who stand against us is *not* invincible and no better proof of that is the manner in which we have over these many years held them at bay, even at times when the odds were still more awesome than they are today. The country is not bankrupt. On the contrary: Per capita Israel ranks among the foremost exporting countries. Its industrial and technical plant and manpower is among the world's finest. Its institutions of higher learning, counting over 55,000 students, are in the best tradition of Jewish intellectual excellence. Israel is very much a going concern. For a country as small and as short of resources its achievements make it a unique success story in which all of us can take justifiable pride. Moreover, beyond the shrill of public debate lies a strong, cohesive, solid, national unity on which rests the entire national infrastructure. Above all there is conviction in our hearts in the justice of our cause for our cause is life for Israel and its people.

Let no one therefore doubt for even a moment that together we can ensure that this coming year will not only be a year of decisions but a year in which the decisions that we shall make, and that others shall have to respect, will be such as to consolidate and fortify a secure and peaceful Israel.

גמר חתימה טובה ושלום על כל בית ישראל.

A Happy New Year, and peace unto the whole House of Israel.

Remarks

Address to the Joint Israel Appeal
London, December 1, 1980

There is a measure of poetic justice in our meeting here tonight. For as *we* gather to mark and to express and indeed to celebrate the universality and totality of our Jewish commitments, others — to be precise the leaders of the European Economic Community — are assembled in Luxembourg in order, one must presume, to further advise Israel of the course which *they* consider it should follow, the decisions it should make and the risks it should take. The significance and timeliness of *our* assembly is therefore that at the very time when Europe deliberates what is best for Israel in the light of what is best for Europe, we have convened in order to resolve and to act on what *we* — the Jewish people — consider is in the best interests of the Jewish State.

In saying this we harbour no malice and mean no disrespect for our European friends. Neither are we really profoundly disturbed or alarmed by what they may propose to say or to advocate. For there is one essential truth that needs to be recalled and restated: It really *is* within the capacity and the power of the Jewish people to chart its own course and to protect and ensure its own destiny. This I believe is what Israel is all about. And this is also what this gathering of ours is all about.

In saying this I am not necessarily referring only to the

challenge of diplomacy. Crucial as this undoubtedly is it must not become the be-all and end-all of our efforts. For far too long have we allowed the business of doing diplomatic and other battles to be the focus of our exertions. Indispensable as these are to our very existence they are but necessary evils to be resorted to in the process of fulfilling our true mission, namely the building and consolidation of a nation and a society that will live up to the norms and ideals of our people, provide a dignified living for its citizens, give expression to the cultural standards that we — and others — have come to expect of us, and altogether combine to challenge and attract the best of our people everywhere to join and partake in our enterprise.

This too is what this gathering is all about. But there is also a practical, immediate purpose to your meeting — namely to address yourselves to an agenda of pressing needs. As you take up this agenda, may I be permitted to urge you not to condition yourselves to think in terms of a *needy* Israel — only of the *needs* of Israel. While these may well be enormous they should not become the central theme of your endeavours. In responding to the continuing needs of Israel you must never lose sight of the miraculous accomplishment that *is* Israel. We may be the repository of the overwhelming majority of the socially and economically deprived of our people, but we are *not* a social case. We may have poverty and slums but that does not mean that we have failed. Rather our situation attests to the manner in which we have provided a haven for multitudes of the needy of our people who have come to our shores while others, somewhat more privileged, went elsewhere. We may have our fair share of backwardness and ignorance, of crime and vice, but then we are also the receptacle of all of the miseries accumulated by the Jewish people in many centuries of persecution and deprivation — from the ghetto to the mellah. We may sound shrill and at times appear rent with dissension but then we are the composite of all the obsessions and the idiosyncrasies of a people noted for being somewhat odd. We may at times seem impoverished and on occasion appear almost destitute — and yet, we and we alone, are responsible and accountable for no less than 96% of our national fiscal requirements which include an unparalleled defence burden requiring no less than 30% of Israel's budget and the servicing of a foreign debt incurred mostly for defence purposes and totalling yet another 30% of our national budget.

For reasons not unrelated to our unique defence requirements, Israel's inflation rate presently leads the world. Grave as it is, this is by no means the only nor the most accurate indicator of our economic fortunes. Consider for instance the manner in which Israel increased its exports this year by 20% — which are expected to reach the phenomenal figure of no less than 10 billion dollars in goods and services of which 5.5 billion dollars are in goods alone of which in turn 85% are industrial goods. Measured by GNP per capita Israel today leads such countries as Italy, Spain and Ireland and is the equal of the United Kingdom. There are few countries indeed that can boast of a technological and scientific base as Israel's industry does and nothing reflects better Israel's achievements in this respect than the fact that close to 30% of its industrial exports now consist of sophisticated products developed through indigenous Israeli research and development.

This remarkable achievement is the vindication of what

91

has been one of our greatest and most remarkable joint efforts — namely a system of higher education consisting of seven universities in which are enrolled this year over 55,000 students. Not bad for a country of three and a half million people when you consider that Britain's total student population is only slightly more than 250,000.

Illiteracy may not yet have been completely eradicated in Israel and yet Israel ranks among the world's leading countries in books published per capita, accompanied if you wish by the chords produced by some of the greatest orchestras and musical ensembles anywhere.

As we have done all this we have had to hold at bay a vast horde of enemies. And not only have we predominated every time we were put to the test — five times in thirty years, but we have also triumphed in the most meaningful sense of the word, in having prevailed upon our former leading adversary to abandon the option of war and to seek the road to peace. Today Israel and Egypt combine in serving as a zone of peace and stability in the Middle East while the rest of the area is in the throes of outright war and bitter internecine conflicts.

These, ladies and gentlement, are but some of the reasons why the Israel that you have been serving is an Israel you can be deeply proud of.

With your indulgence may I end on a somewhat sober note as befits a gathering of the most dedicated of those who labour in the cause of Israel: Israel is presently going through an exceptionally difficult period — perhaps without precedence in our stormy recent history. By the time we emerge from the crucible through which we are presently passing — as surely we shall — we will have accumulated experiences and traumas unique to ourselves.

Therein lies a problem, for inevitably this precludes full partnership with those who have not been affected by them directly.

Let us do our utmost therefore to ensure that when we Israelis are free to look back on these traumatic times, we will be able to draw on the reassuring knowledge that, as we plodded along our present arduous journey, you were with us in support and encouragement, in patience and understanding. Furthermore while we grapple with the awesome agenda that is presently ours, coping as best we can on the one hand with the exacting business of peace-making, and on the other with eking out an economic existence as well as ensuring our physical one, try if you can — on your behalf and ours — to prepare for the day when the present necessarily monetary feature of Diaspora-Israel relations, will concede to something more lasting and meaningful. This may well be the greatest challenge we will ever face together. Thank you.

3

The Middle East

Lebanon: A Commentary

Dutch version published in "NRC–Handelsblad" on June 19, 1979

We live in troubled times: The price of a barrel of oil (which costs twenty cents to produce) on the "spot market" in Rotterdam was last reported to be thirty-seven dollars; the United States has just announced that it will subsidise the purchase of fuel oil by no less than five dollars per barrel; hardly a day goes by without one or another distinguished statesman issuing dire — and timely — warnings about the catastrophic consequences of these trends ("collective suicide" as the French Foreign Minister recently described it); harried officials rush from one capital to another in a desperate attempt to forestall just such a calamity. In practice, however, the only thing everyone seems to have agreed upon is the need to tread softly lest they offend this or that oil producer who might then retaliate by reducing his daily oil production or raising the price of oil again.

No wonder "Israel's friends" in the United Nations — as the NRC reported on May 19, 1979 — are getting "impatient" with Israel. "Israel's friends in the United Nations" have more important things to worry about than its obstinate refusal to accept their own convenient solutions to some of the Middle East's complex problems.

The list of issues on which "Israel's friends in the United Nations" are losing patience with it is long and should, by

97

now, make very boring reading. Let us therefore consider only one of these issues — which for reasons that need not be elaborated upon has for some months now consumed almost as much newsprint and television time as the so-called "energy crisis": Lebanon — the subject of — according to "Israel's friends in the United Nations" and as reported by the NRC — Israeli "stupidity", "arrogance" and "shortsightedness".

As "Israel's friends in the United Nations" would appear to see it, the situation in Lebanon is roughly as follows: From the northern bank of the Litani River all the way presumably to the other end of the country all is blissful. Peace and quiet reign everywhere. The Syrians have long since gone home to tend their fields and orchards; the PLO has restored Beirut to its rightful custodians; Lebanese authority has been firmly re-established and honoured by all. In Beirut the barricades have long since come down, the gutted streets restored and the luxury hotels rebuilt. Even the gambling casinos are back in full swing!

By contrast the situation in the area extending from the southern bank of the Litani to the Israeli border is radically different. Here, and only here, the scene is one of constant violence and bloodshed. The dramatis personae consist first of all of the Palestinians — pastoral and persecuted, defenceless and destitute. Facing them on the other side are the "right-wing Christian militias" — "right-wing" (Fascist), "Christian" (a dirty word in today's Middle East), "Militias" (again echos of Fascism), in short, evil throughout. Supporting these "right-wing Christian militias" is the *bête noire* of them all: the Israelis — ever scheming, ever mischievous. Hovering over all

98

these is the celestial blue of the United Nations — the font of all impartiality and morality.

Alarming as this situation may be, it does nonetheless providentially lend itself to a quick and fairly neat solution: Remove the Israelis and their "right-wing Christian" allies and the blissful tranquility up north could be extended to embrace the tormented south. As simply as that.

This is also how two members of the Dutch Second Chamber seem to have concluded following their recent five-day visit to the "Middle East" consisting of Beirut, Damascus, and for a few hours also Amman.

Our times may well be troubled and our age also the age of distorted truths and warped facts and yet this version of the Lebanese crisis and its possible solution must surely be unacceptable to the average intelligent mind. To begin with there is practically no such thing today as a sovereign independent Lebanon. That Lebanon disappeared in 1976 under the onslaught of the PLO and the tracks of Syrian tanks. The manner in which this came about is best left for the Lebanese to tell. Here is how Ambassador Ghorra, the Lebanese Permanent Representative to the United Nations described it at the Security Council on October 14, 1976:

> [The Palestinians] increased the influx of arms into Lebanon.... They transformed most of the refugee camps, if not all, into military bastions.... Common-law criminals fleeing from Lebanese justice found shelter and protection in the camps.... Those camps in fact became (centres) for the training of mercenaries sent and financed by some other Arab States.... Palestinian

99

> elements belonging to various... organizations resorted to kidnapping of Lebanese... and sometimes foreigners — holding them prisoners, questioning them, torturing them and sometimes even killing them.... They committed all sorts of crimes in Lebanon .... They smuggled goods .... They went so far as to demand "protection" money.... It is difficult to enumerate all the illegal activities committed by those Palestinian elements ....

What is left today of anything approximating a free Lebanon consists of two pockets of predominantly Christian Lebanese, one in an area north of Beirut and the other along the Lebanese-Israeli border. There are those — including some *Christian* politicians — who dislike the Christians of Lebanon and may wish to see them deprived of their last free strongholds. This they are entitled to do. They cannot however take one thing away from their Christian coreligionists, namely their claim to being the only authentic and indigenous inhabitants of the areas in which they have so far been able to hold out. But then these distinguished gentlemen have never met any of these Christian Lebanese or spoken to any of their representatives. Their source of information and enlightenment on the matter is apparently limited to their circle of friends in Beirut. In order to rectify this omission, we would ask to quote the following excerpt from an interview with Father Khassis, Father Superior of the Maronite Order as quoted in *L'Express* on December 30, 1978:

> The grace of accepting martyrdom is not given to everyone. And we have discovered that the Gospel is not as peace-loving as one would have us believe. Self-defence is a law of nature which cannot be against divine law.

100

Even the parable of turning the other cheek to the enemy who wishes to slap it requires that, in order to be able to forgive him, one remains alive. So, you see, one takes one's precautions beforehand." "And," he adds, dreamily, "one's conscience has only the thankless task of justifying what the unconscious has done."

Other than the two predominantly Christian enclaves Lebanon is an occupied country. Its effective master is the 30,000-strong Syrian army. In order to refresh one's memory as to the manner in which Lebanon became an occupied land, it might be useful at this point to quote from a desperate appeal by the International Red Cross on October 5, 1978 for

> ...an end to the slaughter of hundreds of thousands of people in Lebanon. The civilian population, hospitals, dispensaries, public shelters and homes — none have been spared. On behalf of humanity, on behalf of... human right, on behalf of the children, women and old people who are dying by the hundreds, we beg you (the President of Lebanon, world powers, the United Nations and others) to act.

Needless to say nobody acted.

As part of their scheme of occupation the Syrians allocated the area South of the Litani River to the PLO as a base for mounting attacks against Israel across the border. Last year following one such particularly murderous attack, in which all the occupants of a civilian Israeli bus were slaughtered on the Haifa–Tel-Aviv road by a gang originating from a PLO base in South Lebanon, Israel was compelled to move against the terrorist logistical and operational complex there.

In line with traditional United Nations practice once Israel moves — and only then — the United Nations Security Council moves too. Again in accordance with normal Security Council procedure the focus of attention and preoccupation becomes the need to bring about Israel's withdrawal which by now is an established Security Council specialty. Nonetheless, given that Israel did have something to say in the matter of its own withdrawal, on March 18, 1978 the Council finally passed Resolution 425 which called for the immediate establishment of a United Nations Interim Force for Lebanon (UNIFIL) "... for the purpose of (a) confirming the withdrawal of Israeli troops (b) restoring international peace and security and (c) assisting the Government of Lebanon in ensuring the return of its effective authority in the area."

Since then, and again in accordance with established United Nations practice, the only elements of the resolution to be energetically taken up have been those that are not in dissonance with Israel's adversaries. The rest has been relegated to the category of non-feasibility. But then no more can be expected from a United Nations in which a resolution equating Zionism with racism could have been passed.

Not unnaturally therefore the focus of attention ever since has been the elimination of Major Haddad and his "right-wing Christian militias" with hardly any regard for the fate of 100,000 Lebanese, who depend on them for their sheer physical survival. As if *that* were the solution to Lebanon's problem, as if *that* were to put an end to its agony, as if *that* were to restore the "territorial integrity, sovereignty and political independence of Lebanon within internationally recognized boundaries" as called for by Resolution 425. And as if *that* were to bring back the 60,000 dead and the one million refugees (almost *twice* the number which fled from Palestine in 1948).

What then is the solution to the Lebanese problem? Only this: to extricate it from the larger Middle East conflict and thus in a sense restore its traditional status in the area. This is the essential message of Prime Minister Begin's offer to sign a peace treaty with Lebanon, thus achieving this very objective.

Given the intransigence of those who occupy Lebanon today — and one might add the cynicism with which Israel's genuine offer was received by the bystanders — the realization of Lebanese-Israeli peace cannot be expected either imminently nor in the foreseeable future. Its turn will however come within the process of peacemaking initiated and generated by the Egyptian-Israeli treaty, which contrary to Israel's detractors is meant also to pave the way towards a comprehensive Middle East settlement and a solution of the problem of the Palestinians, *including* those living in Lebanon.

Until then Israel will conduct itself in accordance with the following three principles:

a. The need to protect the people of Israel from those who have converted South Lebanon into the world's largest logistical base for terrorist operations. This is a matter of vital Israeli national interest, no less so than the price or the availability of an oil barrel is to others.

b. The commitment to help sustain those Lebanese who

are able to exercise their inalienable right to self-defence. This is the moral imperative of Israel's policy with respect to South Lebanon.

c. The international obligation to cooperate with UNIFIL in the discharge of its mandate as guided by the original intent of Security Council Resolution 425. Much as Israel's assistance to UNIFIL and cooperation with it — without which it could not hope to discharge any of its duties — has hardly ever been conceded or even cursorily mentioned by United Nations reports on the subject, Israel will continue to honour its international obligation in this matter.

In pursuing this policy Israel does not expect accolades from anyone. The lack of support Israel gets is hardly a reflection on the merits of its policy but is owing rather to the norms which guide the general approach to the problems of the Middle East today. These call for the least possible resistance to the lowest common denominator of Arab politics, anything that might incur the wrath of the militant and the violent must be scrupulously avoided.

In this respect the approach to the problem of Lebanon is only symptomatic of a much more alarming phenomenon, the most glaring example of which is the cold reception accorded by Europe to the Egyptian-Israeli peace treaty. It was not entirely surprising therefore that our two distinguished visitors from the Dutch Second Chamber to the Middle East were in such haste to report almost gleefully on their return on "the bitterness in the Middle East over the Egyptian-Israeli peace treaty". By "Middle East" was meant Beirut, Damascus and maybe also Amman but not Cairo and Jerusalem which the two gentlemen did not deign to call on although these happen to be the very parties to the peace treaty.

Much more serious of course are such manifestations of these current norms as the inability for example of the recent NATO meeting in The Hague to agree even on a reference to the Egyptian-Israeli peace treaty as a "major step towards a comprehensive settlement in the Middle East". In fact the treaty was not even mentioned by name while by contrast that watchword "the legitimate right of the Palestinians" was given conspicuous prominence.

The question one would wish to present to all those who dote on such things as the "bitterness in the Middle East over the Egyptian-Israeli peace treaty" is this: Have you really pondered the alternative to the Egyptian-Israeli peace treaty? If so — which could not possibly have been the case judging by the cavalier manner in which it has been shunned — then one might have perhaps also considered the possibility that the most probable alternative to the peace treaty is another Arab-Israeli war. This, one assumes, is an alternative hardly relished by any sane person. For if, God help us, such a war were ever to take place, the chances are that these present "troubled times" of ours would go down in history as idyllic and blissful compared with those which would result from another Arab-Israeli confrontation.

Finally a word to those who like our recent visitors to the Middle East would call for "speaking sternly with Israel" — always in the name of "friendship" of course: Unless you are willing to give your support and your sustenance to that almost miraculous breakthrough towards peace in the Middle East, namely the Egyptian-

Israeli peace treaty, you will have seriously compromised your right to pronounce and pass judgement on any aspect of Middle Eastern affairs. You cannot have your cake and eat it too: you cannot meticulously avoid endorsing the *only* hope for peace in the Middle East for fear of alienating those who would spare no effort to destroy *any* Arab-Israeli peace, and expect Israel to take note of your views and interests. Taking Israel to task for every alleged misdemeanour may perhaps serve in good stead as a useful alibi in the event — God forbid — of a relapse in the peacemaking process. It will not however absolve those who indulge in this from the responsibility of having withheld from the first Arab-Israeli peace that critical support and sustenance which it so urgently and so eminently deserves.

Dangers to Peace in the Middle East

Speech at the Institute of Jewish Affairs
London, July 3, 1980

The recent summit of the leaders of the European Economic Community in Venice may or may not go down in history as an important landmark in Europe's relations with the Middle East and with Israel in particular. It is, however, already very noteworthy for the demonstration it provided of the continued failure of the EEC to meet the crucial challenge of providing an increasingly shaky world economy with some protection against destructive and indiscriminate OPEC price and production manipulation. Commenting on this aspect of the Venice Summit — after first offering accolades for its "achievements" on the Palestinian question — *The Guardian* (June 14, 1980) listed a few of the subjects which somehow eluded similar Community success:

> ...The Europeans were less united on the internal reforms necessary to reinforce their new-found foreign-policy cohesion....
> ...Europe's leaders were even less unanimous on what should be done to combat the rapid deterioration in the world economy.
> ...Despite (the) common recognition of the danger of a synchronised world recession, the summiteers were short of answers to the problem.

...There is no consensus within the Community for an increase in aid to the developing countries, unless it is aid paid for by OPEC...

...Nor will the Europeans go next week to the second Venice Summit of the leading seven industrialised nations with anything resembling a concerted response to the world energy crisis. Certainly, the Nine could agree that OPEC's latest price rises were unjustified. The EEC's energy ministers have also agreed on a list of objectives for reducing their oil imports. But they have not agreed on common means. The Commission's proposals for energy spending, funded by an oil-import tax, lay neglected at the bottom of the Grand Canal.

It is no accident that the EEC summit in Venice should have come up with such a lopsided balance sheet. For there is a direct relationship between the Community's continued obsession with such matters as the Palestinian problem and its inability — or unwillingness — to come to grips with a state of affairs that threatens to plunge the world economy into ever deeper recession leading to ever greater unemployment in the West, and the ever growing impoverishment of the Third World.

The explanation for this anomaly is simple: Since 1973, the EEC has attempted to cope with OPEC's onslaught on the very foundations of world economic stability by opting to recycle vital Israeli interests in return for the good graces of Arab oil producers. "Israel for Oil" — that has been and continues to be the Community's answer to the challenge of OPEC.

So far at least this European policy has not resulted in the slightest amelioration of the world's economic plight.

At the same time there is good reason to fear that in pursuing this policy the EEC may well have embarked on a course which threatens to have the most detrimental effects on the prospects for peace in the Middle East. Moreover the Community may paradoxically be promoting a process which will ultimately endanger that very oil which the EEC has been attempting to ensure for itself by acquiescing in most, if not all, the whims and dictates thrown up by the lowest common denominator of Arab oil politics.

Europeans deeply resent and vehemently reject anything smacking of the charge that their Middle East policy, and especially their growing preoccupation with the Palestinian problem, is determined by the exigencies of their dependence on Middle East oil suppliers. Only the other week a mere allusion to this possibility was rejected in the House of Commons as nothing less than "utter rubbish" and "absolute rubbish". But no sooner was this robust denial voiced than we were provided with a very persuasive and authoritative testimony to the decisive role which Europe's dependence on Middle East oil plays in the formulation of its Middle East policy by none other than a former British Prime Minister, The Rt. Hon. Edward Heath.

Writing in *The Times* of June 19, 1980, on the economic crisis facing the world, Mr. Heath asked: "How can the surplus oil producers be *enticed* to maintain high production rates?" and then proceeded to answer it as follows:

...substantive and sustained indications by the Western countries that they are determined to make progress on the Palestinian problem would make it rather less diffi-

109

cult for the leaders of the more moderate surplus oil producers to maintain high production rates.

Whether or not such policies as recommended by Mr. Heath, and as indeed pursued by the EEC, will in fact prove salutary to the world's present economic ills remains to be seen, though sceptics already abound. Here for example is what the *New York Times,* in a leading article entitled "Leaders at Sea in Gondolas" of June 23, 1980, had to say about such concepts.

> For the sixth straight year, the security, the prosperity and the sanity of the world's industrial democracies are best measusred by one word: oil. And still, as is evident again at the present meeting of their leaders in Venice, their response is drift....
> ...The leaders of the nations assembled in Venice know, even if they will not say so, that they are headed for an unending series of major oil crises. They will either join together to share the sacrifices and manage the risks, or they will drown in currents that no one will ever believe they could not see.

Such, according to the *New York Times* at least, is the sense of unreality which somehow continues to permeate the deliberations on a problem that threatens to plunge the world into a crisis whose dimensions and consequences no one can foretell. Certainly such is the unreality and impracticality that distinguish the ingredients of the EEC's corollary consensus on the resolution of the Middle East conflict and particularly its prescription for the solution of the Palestinian problem.

110

An analysis of the Venice statement on the Middle East suggests the following Community thinking.

The ills and woes of the Middle East are the consequence first and foremost of the festering Arab-Israel dispute. Not only is it the cause of most of the instability there but it is also the major obstacle in the way of the West in its attempts to join hands with its Arab allies in order to thwart and resist the growing Soviet pressure in the area.

The Camp David agreements do not provide the answer because they fail to address themselves to the central issue, namely the Palestinian problem. To the extent that Camp David did attempt to grapple with this problem it was doomed to fail because it did not take into account the indispensable role of the PLO.

While it must grudgingly be conceded that the PLO has made things somewhat difficult by persisting in its commitment to its declared objective of dismantling the State of Israel, it is argued that the only hope of moderating this extreme position lies in exposing it to the reality and test of negotiations. Once faced with the need to make tough political decisions the PLO might well relent and moderate, whereas if it is to continue to be kept out of the peace process it will only be driven into ever more extreme positions.

In the meantime it is necessary to establish the principle of self-determination and to reaffirm the need for Israeli withdrawal from the territories occupied in the Six-Day War, thus delineating both the political and territorial confines within which the Palestinian problem may hope to find its solution.

To redress the serious strategic setback that would be incurred as a result by Israel, the EEC proposes to contrib-

111

ute towards international guarantees including such that will take practical form on the ground. Furthermore, these guarantees are to be hinged on a Security Council Resolution.

In the likely event that such a package will still be unacceptable to Israel, pressure will have to be applied which Israel in its present position will find difficult to resist. So far the European thesis.

How does all this tally with the reality of the Middle East as seen from the volatile Middle East if not from the serene shores of Venice? There is no better demonstration of Europe's deference to the Arab oil producers than the present *European* attempt to establish a link in between the situation in the Persian Gulf and the Arab-Israeli peace process. To argue in these terms and then to proceed to act accordingly is almost guaranteed to ensure that the critical problems of the Gulf are ignored, in order not to deflect Western attention from the true causes of the recent Western setbacks in the area and the dangers which continue to threaten them.

The reason the Russians decided to move into Afghanistan was not because the West was inhibited from deterring them from doing so by the constraints of the Arab-Israel dispute. They did so after taking accurate stock of the steep decline in the West's power and credibility in the Persian Gulf.

To suggest — or worse still to believe — that internal Arab conflicts and conflicts between Arab states can be checked by cutting Jerusalem in half is to shut one's eyes to the root causes of the instability affecting most of the regimes in the area. This stems from a number of *indigenous* causes, primarily the corrosion of what once were puritanical societies by their inundation with Western consumerism and hordes of *gastarbeitern*. The West is misguided if it believes that it can continue to pump millions of barrels of oil a day and then merrily recycle them back into fragile desert kingdoms with the best and worst that the West can offer, without undermining their very foundations. No so-called "concessions" over Jerusalem — assuming they were within Europe's ability to provide — could compensate for that. Nor would the flooding of these countries with all the arms that money can buy along with yet more *gastarbeitern,* not to speak of the possible if not certain consequences of telescoping local youngsters into the cockpits of F-15s.

Worse still: by attempting to establish a direct link between its misfortunes in the Gulf and the ups and downs of the Arab-Israeli peace process, Europe is not only — deliberately or otherwise — misreading the true nature of the problems and dangers in the Gulf. It is also compromising that critical measure of stability which has been created by the Egyptian-Israeli peace treaty at the other end of the region. It is difficult to fathom the considerations and calculations that lie at the bottom of a deliberate effort to establish such linkage unless it is part and parcel of a policy predicated first and last on the need to assuage and placate the oil producers of the Arabian peninsula to the extent of conceding them veto power over the terms and conditions of Arab-Israeli peace. What Europe fails to realise is that in so doing it is also almost certain to guarantee that these same oil producers become active belligerents in the conflict that is bound to result from the collapse of the peace process whose fate Europe now seems willing to entrust to them.

113

The most telling evidence of Europe's increasingly unrealistic position on the Arab-Israel problem has been its reaction to the Camp David agreements and the first Arab-Israeli peace, until only recently considered almost beyond reach. There were some — and Britain's former Prime Minister, Mr. James Callaghan was foremost in this respect — who wisely gave Camp David their warm and generous support. Most of the others preferred to register doubts and reservations: Camp David was "divisive" and therefore destabilising; it isolated Egypt from the rest of the Arab world, which was unwise; it pitted Arab against Arab instead of Arab against Israeli — which was unnatural. Israel itself stood accused of having made a "separate peace" with "only" one Arab country — albeit the leader of the Arab world and, incidentally, also the only one willing to make peace. The enormous concessions it had made in the cause of peace, including the ceding of *all* of Sinai along with airfields and oil fields — not to speak of the strategic importance of the peninsula itself — all these went almost unnoticed while the economic and military burdens resulting from it remain unappreciated. It mattered not that the Camp David agreements came up with a far-reaching formula to tackle that "real" problem of the Palestinians in the form of the proposed autonomy for a five-year "transition period" along with a commitment to discuss the "final status of the territories" towards the termination of that period. This was not good enough for Europe principally because it was not good enough for that host of Arab countries — including all of the oil producers — which reject Camp David and Arab-Israeli peace altogether.

It was therefore only a question of time before Europe

would begin to proffer its own prescriptions for dealing with the Palestinian issue. When finally the first European call went out for a full-fledged Palestinian state and the recognition of the Palestine Liberation Organization as its representative it was, not surprisingly, from a European foreign minister who was soon revealed to have no knowledge of the existence, let alone the contents, of the Palestinian Covenant — the unabashed statement of the PLO's genocidal objectives? So much for Europe and the reality of the Middle East.

What was an obeisant preamble to a commercial agreement between an EEC state and one of its Arab oil suppliers has now become standard European policy as enshrined in an authoritative European statement, appropriately proclaimed in Venice — a classic scene for the enactment of centuries-old European-Jewish tensions and the city where the ghetto originated.

What have the Europeans done in Venice? In proclaiming the right of the Palestinian people to "exercise its right to self-determination" and endorsing the claims of the PLO to "be associated" in the process leading to the realization of that right, while scrupulously avoiding the slightest reference to the PLO's conception of the *manner* in which this right is to be exercised, the EEC has as much as conceded to the PLO its rightful claim to this very conception. Today the PLO has every good reason to assume that as far as Europe is concerned it is entitled to join the peace process with its Covenant *intact*.

In the eyes of those who live and kill by its precepts the Palestine Covenant has now been accepted as a legitimate credo relevant to any international effort towards the resolution of the Palestinian problem. That is the only interpretation that the PLO can be expected to give to a European statement which accedes to every Arab demand — from the territorial issue to the question of Jerusalem — and which denounces the Israeli settlements as a "serious obstacle to peace in the Middle East", yet does not dare to declare the Palestine Covenant at the very least as an *equal* obstacle to peace. What is the PLO or anyone for that matter, to make of a statement in which the only accession to any Israeli viewpoint or interest is a bland endorsement of "the right to existence and security of all the states in the region, including Israel"?

What perfect symmetry: The PLO is accepted as a legitimate interlocutor along with its Covenant in return for Europe's reaffirmation of Israel's right to exist. An organisation of blatant terrorists is accorded the status of statehood and a full-fledged viable and vibrant state is conceded the "right to exist". As if, one might add, Israel's right to exist depended on any other country's good will; as if Israel's existence was ever the responsibility of anyone but its people; as if the perennial attempts to extinguish Israel's existence over the past thirty years were ever repelled by anyone but its citizens' army; as if those who sell massive amounts of arms to countries that persist in their total enmity towards Israel took into account the impact of these arms on Israel's ability to protect its existence.

Is it any wonder that the PLO's reaction to the Venice statement should have been such as to prompt even the *Times* of London to complain that Yasser Arafat "shows a dismal lack of respect for people who are trying to help" (June 14, 1980)? Why should the PLO have been expected to yield any of its totalitarian tenets when until now neither their steadfast reiteration nor their assiduous application has prevented them from gaining growing acceptance and recognition by the EEC? Did not the Europeans extend to it the right of "association in the peace process" less than a week after the most explicit reaffirmation by El Fatah — that allegedly "moderate" component of the PLO — of the Palestinian Covenant's central commitment "to liquidate the Zionist entity politically, economically, militarily, culturally and ideologically"? For once, one wishes that the Europeans had at least emulated Dr. Kreisky who, according to press reports, was so shocked by the El Fatah statement that he withdrew his support for an invitation to the PLO to the forthcoming meeting of the Socialist International. Instead the EEC is preparing to despatch its emissaries in order "to make the necessary contacts" with the PLO — as called for by the Venice statement — when the PLO will be well within its rights to submit the objectives of its Covenant as the first and perhaps the only subject on the agenda. So much for Europe's moderating influence on its newly legitimised interlocutor — the PLO.

As for the impact of present European policies on Israeli thinking, no comment could be more appropriate than that made by Amos Oz, one of Israel's oustanding writers and most outspoken doves. In an article published on May 25, 1980 in the Israeli daily *Davar* Oz had this to say:

> ...perhaps there is something to the argument of the hawks: if the settlements are halted, Israel will still be in the dock because of the Jerusalem issue; if the Arabs get their way in Jerusalem also, they will put forward new claims. Kreisky's Europe will not cease to accuse Israel of intransigence, of suppressing the Arabs, of threaten-

117

ing world peace and the flow of Arab oil. If the Arab world, and particularly the PLO, becomes convinced that they can achieve all they wish even without making peace with Israel and without finally accepting the legitimacy of its existence, then the end will arrive not only for the positions of the doves in Israel, but also for Sadat's policy and for his regime. If the United States is pulled in the wake of Western Europe and demands of Israel not a "reasonable position" but to provide full and immediate satisfaction for the demands of the radical Arabs and of fanatic Islam, then the tragedy of the doves in Israel will be just the prologue to the tragedy of the free world.

Underlying the Venice statement is the new concept of parallelism between "the right to existence and to security of all the states in the region, including Israel" and the right of the Palestinians to self-determination, plus the endorsement of the PLO as a legitimate expression of those rights as well as the vehicle for their realisation. This seems to have been primarily a British contribution to EEC thinking as attested by statements made recently in this very forum by Minister of State at the Foreign Office, the Hon. Douglas Hurd, and which included the following:

[The Palestinians'] right to a homeland, to self-determination and to full participation in negotiating a settlement... must be considered and its application must be negotiated *alongside* Israel's legitimate claim to security if there is to be a just and lasting settlement.

Because it establishes this parity between Israel's claims and those of the Palestinians, now inevitably including

those articulated by the PLO, the Venice statement constitutes the sharpest deviation from the Camp David agreements. Whereas Camp David sought to avoid the head-on
collision of claims which, as a result of Arab extremist
stands over many decades, have tragically become mutually exclusive, the Venice statement seeks to resolve the
conflict by juxtaposing the two claims as equally legitimate
and then proceeding to attempt to resolve the clash
between them. Whereas Camp David strove to establish a
framework for a *gradual* process of reconciliation and
peaceful coexistence, Venice seems to have opted for a
dialectical process of direct confrontation between two
sets of admittedly conflicting claims in the hope of temper-
ing them through negotiations to the point where a mutual
accommodation becomes possible. Daring and novel as
this concept may seem, it is no more than a throwback to
another era when once before violently conflicting claims
were allowed and even encouraged to confront each other
up to and including the test of violence itself. Hence apparently the recent revival in this country of such political
terms as "Palestine", "The Palestine Question" and even
the equation of Arab terrorism with what has been
referred to as no less than "Zionist" terrorism. Much of
the inspiration for this revival probably draws on a chapter
in British and Middle Eastern history that came to a close
thirty-two years ago — and which for everybody's sake is
best kept closed.

Let all who toy with such notions be reminded that we
are dealing here with neither a mandatory situation nor
with a colonial vestige, but with a confrontation that is
already sufficiently lethal without its being made worse by
experiments in Middle Eastern dialectics. Those who

advocate this course together with a return to the polemics and confrontations of yesteryear should consider well the perils and very probable consequences of doing so in the Middle East of today.

Thanks to the combined efforts of the Soviet Union and the West, the Middle East today boasts of the largest arsenals of arms outside the United States and the Soviet Union. If and when the showdown which the PLO and its allies seek and which Europe may unwittingly be lubricating with its policies, does take place, it will involve among other things the deployment, in an area not much bigger than the Salisbury Plain, of no less that 15,000 battle tanks, 3,000 combat planes, thousands of artillery pieces, hundreds of missiles and close to two million troops. These add up to a fire power that is much greater than that of *all* the combatants in Europe combined at any time during the Second World War. The Arab countries today have more and *better* tanks than all of NATO has in Europe. Moreover, if and when that showdown takes place it will involve not just the countries bordering on Israel but every Arab state. This has been rendered inevitable by the supply of weapons to such distant countries as Saudi Arabia which is sure to suck them into the battlefield almost from the beginning. In other words, if and when another Middle East war takes place it will be an all-out *regional* war from which nobody emerges unscathed. That is the prospect which those who run the risk of a final showdown between Israeli and Palestinian must take into account along with the consequences to Europe and the rest of the industrial world.

This is precisely the Armageddon which Camp David was meant to avoid. Camp David was an attempt to build an Arab-Israeli peace on the cornerstone of an Egyptian-Israeli peace alongside an attempt to cope with the Palestinian problem in a measured and controlled manner over a period of five years. In jettisoning Resolution 242 and discarding Camp David, Europe has opted for what it believes is a short cut. But in so doing it may be charting a course towards unimaginable calamities. One thing Europe fails to realise is that whereas the Czechs could opt to accept the Munich dictate in 1938 and the Soviet ultimatum in 1948 and continue to survive as a nation, Israel has no such option. Defeat would mean extermination. But, whereas the Czechs had neither the wherewithal nor the will to fight, Israel has both.

As for Europe's potential for applying pressure on Israel to accept a prescription for Middle East peace which Israel considers as more likely to lead to its demise, Europeans should be the first to know that their leverage on Israel is minimal and therefore "manageable" for more than just "the time being" as has recently been suggested in this forum. Europe has for years abstained from supplying Israel with arms, and, at critical moments, even refused to provide it with spare parts for equipment purchased a few years earlier. The embargo imposed by Britain in the war of 1973 when sorely needed spare parts for British-made Centurion tanks were withheld is one case among several. Similarly, Europe has for years now withheld economic assistance from Israel even when such assistance was as justified as it was following the signing of the Egyptian-Israeli peace agreement. Then, the EEC scrupulously abstained from joining the United States in extending economic assistance to the peacemakers, if only to demonstrate to the warmongers that the making of peace had its economic rewards at least. In Israel's case this was particularly felt in view of the enormous sacrifice involved in evacuating the Sinai oil fields and the cost of transplanting a huge defence infrastructure from the Sinai Peninsula to the south of Israel. A large measure of Israel's present economic distress is owing to its share in the implementation of the Camp David agreements. As for European political support, Israel has for all intents and purposes been deprived of it for some time. The best demonstration of this is the fact that Israel today finds itself almost totally alone in trying to fend off the escalating political warfare waged against it by the Arab world and its allies in the UN, where the only support it can expect, and that not always, is from the United States. What leverage does Europe have over Israel? Certainly not a moral one. Europeans may resent the manner in which Israelis cite the Holocaust as a central feature of Israel-European relations but that does not alter the historical record. In the eyes of the Israelis, Europe is less than well qualified to admonish Israel on moral grounds. In this respect the balance sheet between Israel and Europe will *always* remain heavily in Israel's favour. Other than to make Israel's lot more difficult than it already is, Europe really has no leverage with which to impose upon it any prescription for a Middle East peace that Israel considers to be unacceptable. Unless of course Europe should go the whole hog and place itself squarely behind the Arab rejectionists. Can we be sure that this unlikely option is not being considered?

There really remains very little to say about the proposition that Israel should divest itself of all its basic strategic assets and place its trust in international guarantees including — of all things — "guarantees that may be

122

provided by the United Nations by the decision of the Security Council". Suffice it only to recall how at the height of the Yom Kippur War in 1973 there was not a single European country willing to place a single airstrip at the disposal of a single United States plane carrying vitally needed supplies to an embattled Israel, for fear of incurring the wrath of this or that Arab oil producer. Whereas the United States has shown a readiness to put at risk some of its vital interests for the sake of advancing the overriding objective of Arab-Israeli peace, the Europeans made it patently clear that their sole motivation was that of short-term self-interest. This may seem legitimate in cruel realpolitik terms but it is hardly a good credential for anyone purporting to act as either an objective arbiter or a provider of guarantees.

Mr. Heath may well have done us all a good service by calling a spade a spade and revealing once and for all that the true logic and purpose of present European diplomacy is none other than that which has been already summed up as "Israel for Oil". So be it: let the European-Israeli contest be spared the trimmings of moralistic protestations and be confined to the politics of pure self-interest. But in that case let these also include the following dimension: Small as it is, Israel comprises no less than fifty percent of the Arab-Israel conflict. That conflict cannot and will not be resolved except on terms which Israel considers acceptable. And Israel will accept no peace unless it is one which Israel and Israel alone considers to be a secure peace. Let this too be a point of reference — a central point of reference — for all who predicate their policies on what they perceive to be their self-interest.

Middle East Realities — An Israeli View

Address at the Royal Institute of International Affairs
Chatham House, London, April 22, 1982

Introduction

Views of the Middle East are as numerous and diverse as
the myriad issues and interests associated with this turbu-
lent region. No views, however, are more relevant than
those of the parties perceived as being directly involved.
The Middle East as seen by Israel — which all would
presumably agree is a party centrally involved — may not
be the same as, or even close to, the Middle East as seen by
others, both within and outside the region. To discount
this view, however, is to ignore an essential factor, namely
the perception and assessment of Middle East realities by
one of the major determinants of the issues of war and
peace in the area. Such is the essence of our claim to be
heard and perhaps to be considered and even heeded.

1. *The region overviewed*

Contrary to a fairly wide consensus among governments
and media, Israel does not consider the problem of the
Palestinians as the central issue of our times or even of the
Middle East. Bitter, complex and seemingly intractable as
it is, the Arab-Israel conflict is but one focus of Middle
East tensions and violence among many, and as such not
necessarily the most critical. Consider the state of the

124

region today — April 22, 1982 — clockwise if you please: the Lebanese state continues to lie prostrate, held to the ground by a Syrian army of occupation of over 20,000 soldiers ostensibly to keep the peace between an usurping PLO and a variety of Lebanese factions struggling — when not with each other — to prevent the incorporation of their country into a Greater Syrian state. And may I hasten to anticipate those who must by now feel prompted to expose our own involvement in this sad story, by suggesting that had we not been involved in what is left of Lebanon it would cease to exist altogether. Likewise, whatever prospects exist of Lebanon ever being put together again are contingent on a credible Israeli neighbour powerful enough to deter the Syrian would-be annexationists and thus keep alive the hope of a free Lebanon.

Accross the border in Syria proper prevail brotherly love and bliss. Ask the people of Hamma or those of them who survived the recent carnage. Much as one may try, it would be difficult to establish an Israeli connection with that bloody episode. Rather it would appear that Hafez al Assad considers his internal problems far more menacing even than the diabolical Israelis. How else does one account for his readiness to reduce the city of Hamma to rubble and to inflict on its population no less than 6,000 fatalities, and according to some witnesses up to 16,000. Apart, however, from a recent BBC report and a few other solitary accounts little has been heard of the sacking of Hamma and even less commented on it. Unfortunately it is only when a demented Jew goes berserk on the Temple Mount that world opinion is exercised and the UN Security Council is moved into — fortunately — impotent action.

What happened in Hamma had nothing to do with us and everything to do with the present state of Arab society. Typical as it was of the Assad regime the Hamma episode was symptomatic of a society wracked with internal tensions and conflicts on practically every level of national and communal life.

Further clockwise, on the Syrian-Iraqi border we encounter a classic example of inter-Arab relations in the form of sealed boundaries, ruptured diplomatic relations and reciprocal exchanges of animosity, abuse and mutual subversion. Here we do seem to be somewhat involved considering that both regimes accuse each other of being in the pay of none other than the agents of Zionism as aided and abetted by those of American imperialism.

The next frontier offers very little cause for merriment not only for Sadam Hussein but also for every regime along the coast of the Arabian Gulf — or is it the Persian Gulf after all? Here, at the eastern end of the Middle East — in the Gulf area — decisive facts are presently being created that may have far more bearing on the future of the Middle East and indeed of Europe than whether or not Arafat will or will not concede Israel a conditional right to exist. In view of the gravity of the situation and the issues involved we may be forgiven for suggesting that if only a fraction of the attention and preoccupation that are daily being expended on the Palestinian question were to be invested in a serious consideration of the dangers and opportunities presently being created in the battlefields of the Shatt el Arab, the West might be better equipped to meet the challenge of the Iraqi-Iranian conflict and its exploitation by the Soviet Union, especially if the military situation should begin to approach — as it seems to be doing — a decisive stage. Unfortunately this is not yet the case. With no less than three intelligence fiascos to its credit, namely the collapse of the Shah's Iran, the sudden and unexpected Iraqi attack on Iran and now the no less unexpected turning of the tables on Saddam Hussein, the West — governments and media alike — continues to invest far more time, attention and resources in that all-consuming issue of what to do for, or about, Mr. Arafat, than on seriously pondering the possibility of a Gulf dominated by Ayatollah Khomeini. Not that a Gulf dominated by Saddam Hussein is particularly to be relished.

The Gulf is hardly the only issue that has fallen victim to this curious Western infatuation with the Palestinian question. When the history of these years is eventually written it may well reveal this episode to have been a classic case of self-inflicted massive disinformation. Indeed one cannot but wonder whether this has been a mere accident and not the product of somebody's clever manipulation. In the meantime Israel seems to be seriously implicated in the Iraqi-Iranian struggle, as suggested at least by the manner in which both contestants befoul each other with the ultimate charge of acting at the behest of none other than International Zionism.

Mercifully we seem to be less involved elsewhere. No one at any rate has as yet accused Israel of engineering a recent coup attempt in Bahrein just as we have not been projected as backers either of North or South Yemen in their tête-à-tête at the southern tip of the Arabian Peninsula. We also seem to be absent from the ongoing struggles in the lands along the western coast of the Red Sea and the northern coast of Africa. This is more Qaddafi territory than ours which, however, hardly detracts from its volatility as evidenced by conflict at The Horn, civil war in Chad, bloody confrontation in formerly Spanish Sahara and recurrent attempts at the subversion of existing regimes from the Sudan to Tunisia.

And yet all of this catalogue of strife and woe has not elicited even a fraction of the attention and coverage that has been heaped on the Arab-Israel conflict. But then the Middle East is not the only victim of this obsession with our problem. Other issues much closer and more pertinent to Europe have also suffered. Consider the following, for example: during the period August 31, 1981–February 25, 1982 the BBC World Service — undoubtedly the finest and most influential of its kind — produced no less than *seven* "World Today" programmes in which the main topic was an Israel or Israel-related subject; five more dwelt on similar subjects as sub-topics. In addition to these the BBC World Service broadcast two programmes on the "occupied territories" while seven other programmes included this same subject as a sub-topic. By comparison the BBC World Service devoted over the same period a mere *four* programmes to the subject of "European Security" while five more referred to it as a sub-topic. Jews may well be news but this would appear to be somewhat excessive, even through the Arab-Israel conflict has not exactly ended.

2. *The Arab-Israel conflict*

Arab-Israel relations are marked by two contradictory processes: on the one hand the Egyptian-Israeli peace continues to make progress and an important phase of it will very soon be consummated with the final evacuation of the Sinai by Israel. On the other hand, sadly and paradoxically, Arab-Israel enmity continues unabated, as yet unaffected by Israel's peace with the leading power in the Arab world.

As Israel finally gives up a set of irreplaceable strategic assets to the south it continues to confront an arc of hostility and potential aggression extending from the Mediterranean in the north to the Red Sea in the east. Far from resigning themselves to the inevitability of peace, a formidable host of Arab countries continues to preach, proclaim and prepare for the certainty of war as political and psychological warfare is escalated and as vast reserves of petrodollars are invested in the acquisition of enormous quantities of weapons.

The Arab world today possesses the largest arsenal of arms and armaments outside the United States and Soviet Union — exceeding the collective military strength of Western Europe. In armour, for example, the combined strength of the Arab world — excluding Egypt — is put at some 14,000 tanks. By comparison the total number of tanks at the disposal of NATO is some 17,000. In other words the Arab countries which Israel stands to face in any future Arab-Israeli war already have today almost as many tanks as NATO and half the number of tanks which the Soviets are known to have deployed west of the Ural Mountains and which we are told constitute the single most menacing threat to Western European defence.

This is hardly the only discrepancy in the Arab-Israeli power equation. To it should be added:

a. The unique geo-strategic disadvantage of a country roughly the size of Wales whose major port is within artillery range of Lebanon; whose capital city is almost within artillery range of Jordan and just one minute's flying time from the Jordanian-Israeli frontier and much of whose military infrastructure in the Negev — recently removed there from the Sinai — is within a few minutes' flying time from a fast-growing and massive Saudi military complex in Tabuk.

b. A demographic-economic disparity which compels Israel to anchor its defence in a citizens' reserve army which may have to be called up and sent into war within hours in order to do battle with combined Arab *standing* armies already totalling a million and a quarter full-time combat-trained troops.

c. A disparity of intent whereby Israel must be constantly braced to choose between absorbing a massive first blow and resorting to pre-emptive military action, thus incurring the stigma of having fired the first shot — a dilemma not entirely unfamiliar in this country today. While our adversaries can always count on an automatic chorus of support by a large and varied assortment of parties — including one superpower — any time they may feel the urge to pounce on us, Israel must first be seen to have been bled — preferably profusely — before it can qualify for any measure of international sympathy. The most agonizing decision the late Golda Meir ever had to make was to forgo — in 1973 — the option of a pre-emptive strike across the Suez Canal. While this may not have decisively changed the course of the opening phase of the war it certainly would have saved the lives of many Israeli soldiers. Priority, however, had to be given to the need to prove that we were indeed the victims of aggression although it was abundantly clear that we were about to be just that. And yet when two weeks later Israel succeeded in turning the tables it was told to go away and accept what may well come to be considered the greatest strategic debacle in Israel's history. This is what is meant by the disparity of intent or rather the possible consequences thereof for Israel.

One option decidedly *not* open to Israel is that of sustaining a first blow and then calling on the international community for succour and assistance. Given Israel's unique military, geographic and demographic disadvantages the most we could hope for in such a case would be either prominent space in the obituary columns or compromising with the aggression committed against us, which, in Israel's circumstances would amount to the same thing, if only because any aggression committed against Israel would stand to be initiated not eight thousand but eight or eighteen miles away.

3. *Arab-Israeli peace*

Fortunately, if not miraculously, we no longer need digress only on the realities of Arab-Israel conflicts but can also reflect on the realities of Arab-Israeli peace. We are today on the eve of the completion of the final and climactic stage of Israel's withdrawal from Sinai. Israel's contribution to the attainment of peace with Egypt was never fully appreciated — a fact of life to which we are now almost resigned. There must, however, be no mistake about the traumatic — let alone strategic and political — effects of the tragedy of Yamit and its settlements as of the abandonment of everything else we are leaving behind us in Sinai. Here is a brief list of some of these:

a. Eight airfields, two of which — Eitam and Etzion (near El-Arish and Eilat respectively) are among the

131

world's most modern. Two new replacement airfields have been built in the Negev and a third is on the drawing board. However, problems of aerial congestion, effective dispersal on the ground and the shortage of airspace for training purposes will not easily be solved.

b. Electronic early-warning stations on the Sinai mountains. There is no replacement for these just as there is no compensation for the Egyptian ability now to use these heights for monitoring activities deep inside Israel.

c. The naval base at Ophira (Sharm-el-Sheikh): much as we have faith in Egypt's commitments to ensure freedom of passage through the Straits and in the contribution in this regard of the Multinational Force and Observers (MFO) one cannot entirely discount the possibility of circumstances that could result in yet another blockade of the waterway and a consequent regional if not global crisis.

d. Infrastructure. When Israel came into possession of Sinai in 1967, it found a vast, sparsely populated desert, with a few narrow, poorly maintained roads and hardly any economic infrastructure or facilities. In the firm belief that development of this desert-buffer would, in the long run, be the most effective security against possible future aggression, Israel proceeded to build a network of modern roads — covering over a thousand miles — power lines, water systems and communications networks which today serve the entire peninsula.

In the fourteen years since 1968, Israel spent no less than $17 billion on development projects in Sinai — $10 billion for defence, $5 billion for oil-resources development and $2 billion for roads and civilian installations. Most of this infrastructure, whose value equals that of Israel's entire

foreign debt, is now being forfeited. Staggering new out-
lays must now be budgeted for the relocation of over 170
military camps and installations; the transfer to the Negev
of more than 6,000 buildings of various types and of tens of
thousands of tons of equipment; and the construction of
new settlements, homes, roads, water systems and electric-
ity networks for the large civilian and military population
that has been transplanted.

e. Oil. The western coast of the Sinai Peninsula is dotted
with a chain of oil fields which tap the rich geological
structures beneath the shallow Gulf of Suez. Following the
transfer of the northern fields to Egypt in accordance with
the interim agreement of 1975, the Israeli-discovered and
developed Alma field became Israel's largest single source
of petroleum. By November 25, 1975, when this field too
was handed over to Egypt, its yield had reached two
million tons per year, or 40,000 barrels per day, and considerable scope remained for further development leading
at the very least to Israeli self-sufficiency in energy!

In 1978, Israel spent some $700 million on overseas oil
purchases. Today its annual oil bill has soared to $2.4
billion, a figure roughly equal to the total added value of
the country's present annual industrial output.

It is not as easy to put a price tag on the emotional costs
of the Sinai withdrawal: the uncertainty as to whether or
not the Sinai Peninsula will ever again be utilized as a base
for attack against Israel; the unprecedented uprooting of
towns and villages; the loss of the only "breathing space" a
hemmed-in nation has ever had; the abandonment of religious and historical sites associated with the birth of the
Jewish people. Yet these are the costs most painfully borne
by the Israeli public.

Regrettably the difficulties and traumas experienced by us in completing the final and critical phase of the withdrawal have been compounded of late by a less than helpful Egyptian attitude. We expected — and had every right to expect — a more generous and understanding attitude from our Egyptian partners. This unfortunately has not been the case, resulting not only in embarrassment and disappointment to the Government of Israel at an especially sensitive period, but also contributing to the lingering scepticism and concern among sections of the Israeli public over the future prospects of Arab-Israeli peace.

This Egyptian attitude was not unrelated to the general practice — until now, at least — of laying the blame at Israel's doorstep for every setback or difficulty in the Egyptian-Israeli peace process. What was however widespread practice until now, should in our view be urgently reconsidered. In the first place, it is not warranted. Today's scenes in Yamit and Ophira testify well to Israel's good intentions and its commitment and fidelity to peace. What was, however, at best tolerable until now may well become hazardous after April 25. Taking Israel to task in the liberal manner to which we have — or have not — become accustomed may have very counter-productive results either in encouraging those in Egypt who may wish to argue in favour of disengagement from commitments to Israel under the Egyptian-Israeli peace agreement, or in providing others with an excuse for yielding to pressures that are bound to be put on Egypt as it inevitably and legitimately seeks to revive some of its Arab relationships.

In spite of recent disappointments, we for our part believe and expect that the Egyptian leadership will continue to honour its obligations. In our view, it will — and

134

should — do so for the very best of reasons, namely, vital Egyptian national interests, the most prominent of which would appear to be ensuring against a return to confrontation and conflict; continuing to reap the bounties of peace and maintaining the new and all-important American-Egyptian relationship. However, serious consideration must be given to the possibility that the completion of Israel's withdrawal from Sinai will neutralise what has been until now the chief deterrent against possible Egyptian deviation from the peace agreements. In order to redress this possible imbalance, it is vitally important that all those who truly seek to preserve and further advance the peace process apply themselves to the task of impressing upon Egypt — and indeed upon Israel too — the importance of their peace agreement, for their own sakes as well as that of the entire region.

The Egyptian-Israeli agreement is the linchpin of peace and stability at our end of the Middle East. Regress can lead to collapse, and collapse is too disastrous to contemplate. Conversely, success and vindication should take the peace process forward.

4. *The Palestinians*

Simultaneously with the completion of the withdrawal from Sinai and its traumas Israel is presently engaged in an effort to create conditions for a Palestinian-Israeli dialogue on future co-existence leading to the implementation of the Autonomy Plan of Camp David. Not unexpectedly, the PLO is attempting to disrupt this effort, correctly considering it a threat to its claim to Palestinian leadership. We have every intention of frustrating this PLO attempt. There should be no misunderstanding on this point: there will be no accommodation of the PLO, neither in the peace process nor in the city halls of Nablus or El-Bireh. We will not allow the PLO to sabotage the prospects of the Autonomy, which in our view continues to be the only known and feasible formula for dealing with the problem of the Palestinian Arabs of Judea, Samaria and Gaza and to which we consider ourselves fully committed.

5. *Israel as seen by Israel*

According to a poll just published in Israel some 50% of Israelis would not today have agreed to Israel's complete withdrawal from Sinai, not at any rate from Yamit and its surroundings. This regrettable finding is obviously not unrelated to the present traumatic scenes in Yamit and may well change once this bitter episode is over. At the same time it would be wrong not to see in it a reflection of the general mood of the country as conditioned not just by these recent occurrences but much more so by Israel's experience over the past three years. There is disappointment in Israel, for many of the hopes and expectations that Israelis so naturally and eagerly associated with the signing of the first Arab-Israeli peace have not been fulfilled.

Contrary to prevailing impressions, Israelis too entertained sincere hopes that the Egyptian-Israeli peace would become the first installment in a wider resolution of their conflict with the Arab world and not remain a solitary "separate peace". That this has not materialised has become a source of the greatest disappointment to them. None of us either wish or relish endless conflict. There is no

136

more fervent hope and prayer in our hearts than for peace with our neighbours, if only they would come forward and engage with us in dialogue and negotiation.

There were hopes for a respite from international pressures which among other things would enable the country and the people to tackle the problem of the Palestinians as called for by the Camp David agreements and in accordance with the time frame provided by them. Instead Israel has been subjected to an onslaught almost unprecedented in its history. The concessions that were made, the risks that were incurred, were all given short shrift as Israel was served with an assortment of writs and prescriptions on what it should do next. Having lived up to all of their commitments towards Egypt and fully expecting to be allowed to consummate the rest of the Camp David formula, the Israelis found themselves being told that now that they had acquitted themselves well and pulled out of Sinai in accordance with Camp David, they should henceforth accept formulae and prescriptions hammered out not in negotiations in Camp David but in places like Venice.

The essence of Venice was a formula whereby Israel would be expected to trade literally all of its defensive capacity for a set of international guarantees and a military presence on the ground in which Europe would be willing to participate. At the risk of making allusions to a dispute on which we do not wish to take any public position but at the same time are somewhat emboldened to do so by the manner in which others have drawn parallels between that dispute and some of our problems may I, with respect, suggest the following: it really is asking a lot of a country and people under the constant threat of

137

sudden deadly onslaught, to barter the only means known to them of beating back such an onslaught, for the promise of international guarantees plus some symbolic military presence, and should that prove insufficient presumably also the possible despatch of a flotilla. The surest guarantee of such a flotilla finding itself with no more to do than to pick up a mere handful of survivors, is for Israel ever to accept anything even remotely approximating the formula proposed by Venice.

There were hopes of an easing of the defence burden. This too has failed to materialise. On the one hand the cost of transplanting a vast infrastructure from Sinai to the Negev proved to be far greater than ever anticipated and quite beyond Israel's limited means. On the other hand the country found itself compelled to engage in a renewed and futile arms race as the Arab countries' unlimited financial resources were matched by a propensity to satisfy all their wishes. With the price tag of even the most modest effort to keep up with this arms race added on to Israel's new energy bill, the inevitable result is a three-digit inflation rate. Much more disheartening has been the realization that peace with Egypt has not entirely liberated Israel from the spectre of another conflagration as actual and potential adversaries show every indication of seeking to acquire credible offensive capacities independent of Egypt.

Most damaging however has been the psychological setback. One cannot convert Camp David into a dirty word and expect Israelis to turn a deaf ear. One cannot dismiss all the sacrifices that have been made by Israelis and expect them to relish the idea of doing more of the same. Above all, one cannot expect to tell Israelis that now that they have given up their foremost strategic asset in the

Sinai they should proceed to divest themselves of the rest of their security wherewithal and acquiesce, to boot, in the establishment in their very midst of an entity sworn at the very least to the destruction of their state.

All these setbacks and disappointments have not however been without benefit. Disappointed as it may be, Israel today is also disabused of considerable illusions and misconceptions and is much the better for it. Appearances of discord and disarray to the contrary, the country is resolved, perhaps as never before, to protect what it considers to be prerequisites for its security and well-being. The essence of these is ensuring to the maximum degree possible that *Israel is able to defend itself by itself.* That is not just the only formula known to us for coping with the objective constraints of our unique situation but also the lesson drawn from these recent difficult years. The world we live in, in the Middle East, is no less harsh than others but rather more so. Unlike the situation with others, aggressions when committed against us take place not thousands of miles away but in the very midst of our towns and cities, villages and hamlets. We have neither strategic depth to withdraw to nor room for protracted diplomatic manoeuvrings. Our confrontations are decided in a matter of hours, if not minutes.

Such is the Middle East as seen by us at least and such is the manner in which we propose to grapple with it. Others may see things differently and others still may wish to pit their perceptions and prescriptions against ours. Whatever else this may achieve, it will not serve the cause of peace but rather exacerbate tensions and arouse temptations best resisted.

There is another course of action which has not yet been

seriously considered and which we would wish to commend. And that is the option of noting and registering as a valid Middle East reality, the fact that Israel too has some very crucial national interests and that it is also the best judge of how to protect them. To be allowed to do so is in essence all we ask.

4

Israel and the Middle East

On Peace and Security

The Hague, 1978

As a result of the dramatic visit of the President of Egypt to Jerusalem and the equally dramatic reception accorded to him by the people and Government of Israel, the search for peace is being pursued for the first time since the establishment of Israel on a basis of mutual recognition and publicly professed desire to achieve true peaceful relations at least between Israel and Egypt — the leading power in the Arab world. This is not only as it should be but is long overdue, for there is no way in which peace can be achieved by any two parties unless it is first firmly, clearly and publicly anchored in both parties' undertaking to accept, respect and honour each other's right to exist in peace and security. Let us not forget: Dramatic and courageous as President Sadat's visit to Israel was and as critically important to the prospects of peace as it may be, it was no less also an act in which a 30-year-old wrong was finally put right. That wrong was the denial by Egypt of Israel's right to peace and mere existence. That wrong — that grievous wrong — is still practiced and publicly paraded in most of the Arab world.

Putting an effective end to a 30-years' war will not be easy nor will it be accomplished overnight. Similarly it will not be achieved by either threat or intimidation. Peace will be achieved through honest negotiations and a growing

143

understanding of each partner's genuine and imperative needs.

It is not for us to state what Egypt's needs are, though it would appear that its number-one requirement is peace. Peace would enable Egypt to shift precious resources from the debilitating and futile business of war to the task of providing an exploding and impoverished population with food, shelter and the basic social services that are essential to the most minimal standard of decent life. That is what Egypt requires from Israel: the opportunity to dedicate itself to peaceful development which is not possible unless an end is put to its conflict with Israel. This Israel is willing to grant Egypt fully, unreservedly and wholeheartedly, for we want to put an end to the conflict at least as much if not more than they do. However, we for our part need more than that: we need the fulfilment of certain basic security requirements without which peace alone might prove far too risky and fragile than we could afford and for very good reasons. Let me enumerate some of these:

1. Unlike Egypt it is Israel which has been the victim of no less than five wars in 30 years of Arab aggression against it.

2. Unlike Egypt it is Israel which will still have to contend, for who knows how many years, with the enmity of a considerable part of the Arab world supported by other parties cynically exploiting a tragic conflict in order to advance their own interests.

3. Unlike Egypt it is Israel whose Jewish population is only 3 million whereas that of the Arab world totals 120 million.

4. Unlike Egypt, Israel cannot maintain a large army under arms ready to move at a moment's notice but has to

rely for its defence principally on an army of reservists which have to be called up, equipped and armed and transported to the front line in the event of a surprise attack by a large Arab standing army when minutes can be decisive or even fatal.

5. Unlike Egypt, Israel's territory is small and thus the airspace at the disposal of its air force, on which Israel relies for its very survival, is severely restricted. Such factors as airfields for Israel's air force are therefore not a mere technicality, they are crucial to the country's defence.

6. Unlike Egypt, Israel must find a suitable safeguard against a situation in which a potential aggressor could move unhampered from the Sinai peninsula to the tip of the Gaza Strip, 35 km from Tel-Aviv.

7. Unlike Egypt, Israel does not command the blind political support of scores of nations in the UN where every pro-Arab resolution is passed automatically and any one favorable to Israel is hardly ever even put to the vote.

8. Unlike Egypt, Israel cannot count on third parties to move in to save its armies from collapse and swiftly arrange a suitable Security Council Resolution to that end.

9. Unlike Egypt, Israel is a democracy in which national policy is the expression of the national consensus and not the private, personal decision of a single leader.

10. Unlike Israel, Egypt is a country in which the most charismatic and powerful leader can still disappear overnight and make way for a new charismatic leader who could count on being able to garner public support for himself and for any policy he may wish to pursue.

11. Unlike Israel, Egypt is a country where public opinion can swing full circle at any time.

12. Unlike Egypt, military defeat for Israel does not

145

mean occupation or cession of territory but outright annihilation.

These are only some of the reasons why Israel must insist on minimal security requirements under any peaceful settlement.

There is therefore only one course to follow and that is the course opened up by President Sadat himself, namely that of negotiations. The purpose of these is not to provide a framework for bargaining oriental-bazaar style but to provide an opportunity for the two parties to listen to each other, to try to understand each other's problems, needs and requirements and then jointly find the will and the way to mutually accommodate and satisfy these needs and requirements. This will not happen overnight and neither will it be a smooth process. Let no one panic or be driven to act hastily every time a breakdown takes place.

Above all let no one expect Israel to provide all the concessions and make all the sacrifices. True and genuine negotiations are a two-way street and President Sadat has yet to make the first tangible concession. He could do so by recognising and respecting some of Israel's very real security needs and concerns.

Commitment and Non-Alignment

Speech at the Meeting of the Board of Deputies of British Jews
London, October 21, 1979

Everyone has had his conference. It is our turn now to have ours, and it is my duty to report to you on the state of our "joint party": Israel.

There are two central facts about Israel today: First the degree to which it has become the object of one of the most obscene international onslaughts in recent memory, and second the manner in which it continues to thrive and prosper and above all to doggedly pursue the search for peace despite this massive offensive against it.

I have used the term "international onslaught" advisedly, for it is very much an international effort involving a wide and bizarre assortment of nations and states that seem to have little in common except this hostility towards a small country of three million people — the Jewish state of Israel.

Seldom if ever has any country and people had to face such an array of foes and detractors as Israel does today. Seldom has Israel found itself in such a predicament. Let me cite some of the facts and features that make up the reality that Israel confronts today.

My first reference involves a place which is geographically very remote from our part of the world — Cuba. That is where the leaders of the so-called non-aligned nations recently met in order to pronounce on the state of the

147

world as seen from that so-called non-aligned capital of Havana. They discussed every conceivable subject, and above all heatedly debated the course of the movement over the next three years during which time its rotating capital is to be none other than that same Havana. There was considerable discord and dissent but there appears to have been one subject about which agreement was easy and which, judging by its dominant place in the final communiqué of the Conference served almost as the cement that glued all the other disparate elements together. Israel: that was what seemed to have bridged the chasms. Here are just some of the things they had to say about us in Havana, Cuba, last month as they were inscribed in that final communiqué.

The heads of state or government reaffirmed that racism including Zionism, racial discrimination and especially apartheid constitute crimes against humanity.

The Conference calls for the elimination of colonialism, neo-colonialism and racism including Zionism.

The Conference recalls the Resolutions adopted by the UN and reaffirms the resolutions of the non-aligned which determined that Zionism is a form of racism and racial discrimination, etc., etc.

The Conference denounces the Zionist occupation and usurpation of Palestine and calls for an independent Palestinian state in Palestine. It reaffirms that the city of El Quds must be evacuated in its entirely and restored unconditionally to Arab sovereignty. And it appeals to members to take firm measures, including severance of diplomatic and economic relations with countries which recognised formally or by implication the City of Jerusalem as the capital of Israel.

The Conference invites the Security Council to impose sanctions on Israel and affirms the commitment of its members to the adoption of steps within the UN to confront continuing challenges by Israel including such things as total embargo and sanctions and exclusion from the international community, warning all countries that support the Zionist racist regime, etc., etc., etc.

No less than 95 signatures were attached to this document. Ninety-five nations endorsed all these articles concerning Israel! Admittedly not all really meant what they subscribed to and yet — and this is perhaps the most depressing aspect of this episode — none had any compunctions about doing so in broad daylight for all to witness. No shame, no remorse. *All* joined in this pitiful kangaroo court.

Perverse as they were, Castro's words were hardly in dissonance with much that is being said about us today in the UN — the scene of an annual verbal offensive against Israel — this year more than ever before. By the time the present UN session ends it will have deliberated Israel in every committee and sub-committee of the organization, and it will most probably have overwhelmingly passed no less than forty resolutions condemning and censuring Israel for an endless and mindless list of concocted and fabricated crimes. It will also have knowingly and consciously endorsed in a variety of ways the position and objectives of a murderous organization committed to the destruction of Israel. A similar scene with identical trappings will then be repeated in every UN specialized agency with UNESCO heading the list. Everywhere the war cry this year more than ever will be "Zionism is racism".

Again the UN General Assembly: this time, however, closer to home. The voice of those of whom one has the right to expect sanity and responsibility, and insofar as Israel is concerned, also of morality. The voice of Europe. The voice of a continent that either witnessed or actually took part in the greatest crime in history — the wholesale slaughter of most of its Jewish communities. The voice of a continent which is today the vast graveyard of a third of the Jewish people. A graveyard with no graves and no tombs — so total was the annihilation. The voice of a continent that should know better, that claims to know better.

What did Europe have to say at the sight of this unbridled assault on the Jewish state of Israel? Did it stand up and cry "shame"? Did it rise and call "cease and desist"? Did it extend a consoling hand to beleaguered Israel? On the contrary: it could not even bring itself to run the risk of making special reference to that most miraculous event of the year — the Egyptian-Israeli peace treaty. The first Arab-Israeli peace became, in the EEC statement before the UN Assembly, merely one of a number of mysterious recent "major developments". That was all that Europe, as represented by the present chairman of the EEC Council of Ministers, would deign to say about the arrival of Israel at its first haven of peace.

It is a source of wonderment nearing incredulity to us that such should have been the response of Europe to the Egyptian-Israeli peace treaty. I have alluded to the moral aspects of Europe's skepticism and aloofness towards the treaty from the very day on which it was announced that

150

there was to be peace between Egypt and Israel after 31 years of conflict and no less than five wars! But then perhaps moral considerations should not be expected to count very much after all. What however, of the pragmatic, power-political national-interest considerations? Could this be Europe's response to what is not merely the first but also the most important Arab-Israeli peace, namely between the two militarily most powerful countries in the area? Could Europe not see that in making peace between them Egypt and Israel were attempting to put a cap on that most dangerous of present conflicts in the world's most volatile area? Could Europe not realise that in making peace between them Egypt and Israel were creating a measure of regional stability hitherto unknown in the Middle East and in which Europe must surely have such a vital stake?

One would have expected — and indeed did expect — that Europe, of all political communities, would be the first to grasp the measure and promise of the Egyptian-Israeli peace if only for its own well-being and prosperity. One would have expected Europe to understand how important it was to endorse the peace politically, and to help build and consolidate it through practical economic support in order to help the peacemakers rehabilitate their war-weary economies much as Europe itself was helped not so long ago and thus spared collapse and communist oblivion. In so doing it could have helped not only to protect the peace against those who would seek to destroy it but also offer an important inducement to others who may have been weighing the possibility of joining the peace process and whose involvement is so important to its consolidation and expansion.

151

Instead it is the peace-wreckers who are increasingly being given succour and comfort through a growing tendency to accommodate their dictates, while their keen appetite for ever more arms and armaments is satisfied with hardly a murmur; all of which does nothing more than give them further reason to conclude that it is they who are on the right track.

Is it any wonder that the peacemaking burden has become as heavy as it has? Is it any wonder that Israel's strained economy is now stretched to the maximum as it finds itself not only required to build almost overnight a defence infrastructure in the Negev, but at the same time it is compelled to acquire ever more arms in order to counteract the flood of new arms into the arsenals of those who persist in maintaining their enmity towards it?

Is it any wonder that given these enormous pressures piled as they are on top of the permanent and unique constraints of its situation, Israel should often have to so agonize over decisions required of it? And is it any wonder that Israel should also find it necessary to resist the pressures to make it acquiesce in solutions which it knows to be fraught with the gravest of dangers? And it is Israel alone that has the right to determine what it can live with and what it cannot live without. To those who say that there will be no lasting peace in the Middle East unless it is accepted by the vast majority of the Palestinians we say: There will be no lasting peace or any other kind of peace in the Middle East unless the vast majority of the people of Israel agree to it. Is this any wonder?

Given Israel's present circumstances — which must surely be unparalleled — the wonder is that Israel should continue to function as well as it does. Let no one be deceived or alarmed by the noise and clatter of national debate nor by the frantic prognostications of the statisticians. Israel's body politic is as healthy and strong as it has ever been. Unlike many of those presently congregated at the United Nations in New York, we in Israel first debate our problems publicly and freely and then take our decisions democratically. It may not seem the most efficient system and at times can be quite exasperating, but it is still the best that civilised man has been able to devise. We will not be hurried and we would certainly expect those who together with us make up that small band of free democratic societies, to be patient and respectful of our admittedly cumbersome national decision-making process.

Such phenomena as a three-digit inflation rate may well seem alarming and yet again this is not a true measure of our economic well-being. The yardstick by which to judge our economic performance is the fact that we are just now beginning to emerge from a thirty-year war during which we have had to expend every available — and non-available — resource on what has undoubtedly been an unprecedented feat of national defence. Moreover, the transition from three decades of war and siege requires, in our case at least, an enormous expenditure on the reallocation of a defence infrastructure in which we had to invest over the past twelve years no less than four thousand million pounds sterling. The assistance now promised us by the United States will cover only a fraction of the cost involved. The rest is reflected in great part by that three-digit inflation figure. And let us not forget: as it does all this, Israel — a nation of just over three million Jews in a country singularly devoid of natural resources — continues to hold at bay a horde forty times its number and in command of the greatest treasury of all time, as well as the most precious commodity of our time. And this little Israel produces its own supersonic planes and its own missile boats and its own battle tanks and surely the finest of warriors. That, along with an agriculture that is second to none and an industry as technologically advanced as few others are, is the true measure of our economic performance.

Above all: we have triumphed! We have made peace with our former leading adversary. Let those who wish to do so continue to belittle this almost miraculous accomplishment. Let us however recognise and realise the magnitude of our success: we have begun to turn the tide of Arab enmity. Egypt — the age-old centre and crossroads of the Arab world — has accepted and clasped our hand in peace. A whole theology of denial and enmity has thus been challenged and we fervently hope also begun to be rejected. An age-old bitter conflict may well be in the process of resolution. A heart-rending bloodletting may finally have come to an end. That is the point in time and station in history at which we have arrived. That is the true and full measure of our achievement.

The problems that still face us are immense; our enemies are still legion, but there is confidence in our hearts that having come this far we shall not lack the courage, the wisdom and the fortitude to continue to extend and expand the peace and its blessings until before very long it will also embrace all those whom history, geography and fate have placed astride that little river which flows between the Great Desert and the Great Sea.

Mr. Chairman, Ladies and Gentlemen, fellow delegates: I move a note of confidence and pride in our party: Israel.

Thank you.

154

Reflections Upon the Signing of the First Arab-Israeli Peace Treaty

Dutch version published in "De Tijd"
Amsterdam, June 1, 1979

There was an air of sobriety in Israel the day the Egyptian-Israeli peace treaty was signed in Washington. Israelis were generally described as "reserved". Hopeful yet under few illusions. Not pessimistic yet very realistic. There are a number of factors which would seem to account for this reserved mood: It had been a long conflict and much of it is still very much intact in spite of the signing of the peace treaty with Israel's former most prominent adversary (somehow and significantly the term "enemy" no longer seems appropriate). Ironically and sadly the prospect of an Egyptian-Israeli peace appears to have highlighted once again the implacable and mindless enmity of much of the rest of the Arab world — a very sobering reminder for Israelis on the momentous day of peacemaking with Egypt.

The active endorsement and open encouragement of the cool reaction to the possible dawning of peace in the Middle East by a mighty superpower, admittedly never noted for philosemitism, has hardly given Israelis reason to lighten their mood. By the same token Israelis could hardly be expected to draw much encouragement from

155

Europe's uninspired response to the signing of a peace treaty between Israel and Egypt — after 31 years of bitter and seemingly endless conflict! How ironic that Europe — that vast graveyard of no less than one third of the Jewish people — could not bring itself to give its unqualified blessing to the first Arab-Israeli peace!

For many Israelis the first glimpse of peace was also a poignant reminder of the price that had been paid: all those who were not spared to witness and savour the coming of peace and without whose supreme sacrifice there would have been neither peace nor the state of Israel itself. It has not only been a long conflict involving no less than five Egyptian-Israeli wars (Egypt alone fought in every Arab-Israeli war, while the others always managed to sit out at least one war!) but it has also been a very· bloody conflict and the losses on both sides have been heartrending.

By no means unnoticed or forgotten by Israelis on this day were the enormous strategic and economic sacrifices made by Israel over the arduous and protracted negotiations: The complete withdrawal from Sinai along with the strategic depth afforded by its expanses; The prospective abandonment of a network of airfields so critically important to Israel's air force, the mainstay of the country's defence; The eventual withdrawal from Sharm-El-Sheikh, the flashpoint of two wars and the place from which the passage to and from Israel's southern approaches can be either protected or denied; The ultimate abandonment of the Rafiah settlements and the strategic wedge they were to have provided between Sinai and Gaza and last, but certainly not least, the Sinai oil fields which promised to provide all of Israel's requirements within two to three

156

years. These are enormous sacrifices by any yardstick, and the risks seem all the more formidable given Israel's unique circumstances and the violent vicissitudes of Middle Eastern life.

Israelis were equally aware on this day of national stock-taking of the long and precipitous climb that still awaits them as they set out on their way towards peace. Nobody is under any illusions in Israel and in spite of all those who persist in suspecting them of secretly plotting to the contrary, the Israelis sincerely and genuinely desire a comprehensive settlement, being only too aware of the fragility of a partial one.

For Israelis to have been so reflective on what it is hoped will ultimately be considered the second most important day in contemporary Jewish history — the first one being Israel's Day of Independence — was not really all that unnatural and unwarranted given their singular situation and background. To have acted other than soberly on this day might well have been not so much unbecoming as imprudent.

There was and there still is, however, another very good reason for Israel's subdued and cautious bearing these days, the first days of peace with Egypt. This, however, has more to do with Israel's experience in the long months of the actual peacemaking than with the outcome itself. Israel's experience over the past eighteen months has been nothing short of dismal. In saying so no aspersions whatsoever are being cast on our Egyptian partners to the negotiations. On the contrary: President Sadat and his aides have proven themselves to be tough negotiating partners who have done better for Egypt than anyone would have contemplated or had reason to expect. They certainly got more out of Israel than most Israelis ever thought possible. In achieving all this for Egypt they have however at no time performed and acquitted themselves other than honourably. What has been downright depressing has been not Israel's experience with Egypt and President Sadat but rather its treatment at the hands of the onlookers. For months on end it has been subjected to a cacophony of censure and abuse, ridicule and contempt, threats and warnings, pushing and shoving like no other state in recent memory. No Israeli position was accorded any validity, no argument any serious consideration, no dilemma any understanding and no sensitivity any respect.

Very conveniently — almost surgically — the case against Israel has been articulated as a consequence of Israel's own misdemeanours. It is Israel which is responsible for the defection of so many of its friends. It was Israel's "intransigence", "implacability", "aggressiveness", "fanaticism" and "expansionistic designs", which earned her the condemnation and ostracism that has been her recent lot.

Thus Israel's desperate struggle for *tangible* security, i.e. security anchored in concrete and substantive terms rather than, say, other people's good will or guarantees, is grounds for her condemnation as "expansionist". Others may maintain air and naval bases thousands of miles away from their national territory while Israel is expected to withdraw to lines that time and again were proven to be indefensible. Others may predicate their national strategies on the untrustworthiness of their former allies while Israel is called upon to be oblivious of the continuous belligerency of its present enemies. Others may correct their balance-of-payments accounts and bolster their economies with the aid of massive arms exports, while Israel is supposed to disregard the impact of these very same arms sales on its most vital security. Others may deploy their far-flung fleets in response to the vicissitudes of the Middle East — the world's most volatile area — while Israel is expected to behave as if it was all happening in some remote parts and not within minutes' flying time from its exposed small and densely populated heartland. Others may seek the comfort and shelter of military pacts and alliances while Israel is denied the right even to an independent assessment and determination of its own unique security needs.

Thus the passionate devotion of Israelis to the call and heritage of the Bible is denounced as bigotry. Everyone else is entitled to live by "The Good Book" except the "People of the Book" — those whose national odyssey it chronicles and whose mores and values it enshrines. Others may revel in their great historical figures, while ours are converted into characters in some universal folktale and we are denied the right to bask in the glory of their exploits and conquests. The prophets of Israel, those echoes of Jewish national anguish and voices of Jewish national hope, are adopted as everybody's international philosophers while the people unto whom they were assigned are castigated for taking their prophecies seriously. "Judea" and "Samaria" are good enough terms for Bible-reading sessions but taboo as proper designations for historic provinces of the Land of the Bible and their use by Israeli authorities condemned as an expression of dangerous chauvinism while that artificial term "The West Bank" is almost sanctified. Others may have their religious eccentricities, but not Israel. I shall not easily forget being

159

told some months ago by a self-professed "friend of Israel" that as far as he was concerned, Israel risked losing his "friendship" because of the proliferation in recent photographs from Israel of "little men with little beards". I recall how at the time this brought to my mind other photographs of other "little Jewish men" having their "little beards" plucked by very clean-shaven and very big men in German uniforms somewhere in Europe during the early forties.

Thus an impeccable record of respect for human rights in circumstances of unique national stress has been trampled by a deliberate and systematic campaign aimed at casting doubt on Israel's very morality and so exposing her further to public harassment and flagellation. Such ends apparently also justify every means. Consider for example the cover photo on a *Pax Christi* publication dedicated to the alleged enormities of Israeli barbarism towards the Palestinians, depicting an Israeli soldier pointing his gun at a defenceless Arab farmer — and which turns out to be nothing but a shabby photomontage. Just like its contents.

Thus the passionate and desperate fidelity of an ancient people to the world's oldest movement of national liberation — Zionism — renders it guilty of nothing less than the crime of racism. Others are entitled to the fullest expression of their national uniqueness (whether they possess any or not). A people of whom it was said over 3,000 years ago: "lo the people shall dwell alone and shall not be reckoned among the nations", is denied this expression. Others whose national consciousness and identity are limited to a name-plate in some dubious United Nations forum may profess and savour all the national attributes which they may or may not be able to contrive, a people whose loyalty and fidelity to its national origins, ancestral home and historical records makes it unique in the annals of nations, is condemned for doing the same. Anyone with a few coral reefs under his feet may lay claim to an anthem and a flag, not so a people whose national experience for no less than two thousand years has been the cruellest testing of its resolve to continue to survive as a nation in the face of all odds and adversities. To have triumphed and survived this most frightful of recorded national trials and to have proclaimed at the end of it once again the right to Jewish national expression — Zionism — is considered tantamount to racism as was in fact decreed by that most cynical of conclaves — the United Nations.

And thus when peace is miraculously at hand the Prime Minister of a people who in spite of it all have jealously preserved and protected "Shalom" as the most sacred of their values, is deemed by many of the self-righteous paragons of public opinion to be undeserving of the Nobel Prize. *Pleading* for peace for 31 years does not entitle Jews to a peace prize. The willingness to finally consider their plea apparently does!

But fear not, O Israel, for in spite of thy sins and thy travesties there are still those who while very critical and displeased with you nonetheless concede you the "right to exist"!

Apparently this has little to do with the fact that Israel is a nation-state of three million Jews. It also seems to be totally unrelated to the manner in which those three million Jews who live in Israel have created a state that is the most stable and viable democracy in the whole continent of Asia. It is quite irrelevant that this democratic state

161

happens to be the home of some of the finest institutions of research and higher learning, the scene of some of the liveliest artistic, cultural and literary creativity and in none other than that same unique national language which has somehow managed to survive along with its ancient people. It also seems to be unconnected to Israel's universally acclaimed social experimentations and innovations (remember the kibbutz?) nor to the fact that Israel is credited with being one of the world's three "agricultural powers" while its industry and technology seem to place it among some of the leading industrial countries. It certainly has nothing to do with the manner in which for years now Israel has been in the forefront of those nations whose experience in nation-building has been sought by scores of the world's new nation-states, including many who have been blackmailed into rupturing their diplomatic relations with her. All these apparently are no yardstick for national *raison d'être*. To wit the fact that over fifty percent of the world's one hundred and fifty nation-states possess none or very few of these attributes. Be that as it may, count yourself lucky, O Israel, to be considered at least as worthy of "the right to exist". Just like the Maldive Islands or maybe even Qatar and Dhubai! Or is that asking too much?

For the sake of argument *only*: What is it then which justifies our "right to exist"? One possible clue lies in the reassurance which was recently cited to me that "Israel is safe so long as people remember the Holocaust". In other words as long as the state is seen as recompense for the moral depravity of others. This is of course totally repugnant as a moral premise and without the slightest foundation historically. All those who stood by while the people of Israel almost perished during the war years also stood by later when reborn Israel was threatened with extinction on the very day of its rebirth and did so again every time that threat menaced in later years. We cannot forget how in 1973 American planes carrying supplies to Israel could find no place in Western Europe in which to refuel. (And then there is always of course the danger of being denied the "right to exist" should the number of Israeli beards reach unacceptable proportions!) But all this of course is only for polemics' sake. Israel requires nobody's approbation for its existence just as it has not the slightest intention of entrusting it into anybody's hands but its own. Existence is the very essence of Israel's being. It is the central logic of its history and the promise of its future. In a word: "Am Yisrael Chai" — The People of Israel lives! It really is as simple and categorical as that!

These have been some of the circumstances in which Israel has had to negotiate a peace treaty with its leading Arab neighbour. Why has it been so? And why will it probably remain so? One explanation that comes to mind is that which is also offered by a prominent Israeli historian, Shmuel Ettinger of the Hebrew University in Jerusalem in his recent book *Antisemitism in the Modern Era:*

The establishment of a Jewish State has not weakened the tensions between Jews and non-Jews. Likewise there has been no weakening of the tension and the hostility along with the stereotypization and the attempt to apply the negative individual image of the Jew to the Jewish Collective. In other words that hostile tension which is the legacy of European history is transplanted to the present and allowed to fall on the Jewish

Collective. It is clearer today than ever before that antisemitism and anti-Zionism are nothing but one and the same. Furthermore anti-Zionism is a direct historical and psychological continuation of antisemitism. There is therefore no reason to assume that the existence of a Jewish political centre, the existence of actively directed collective Jewish political and social action will break the continuity either of sterotypization or of the centrality of Jews in people's consciousness. If in the past it was necessary to invent the "Elders of Zion" — those who dwell clandestinely and who meet once every year in the old Jewish cemetery in Prague in order to plan Jewish machinations for taking over the entire world — there is no longer any need for that.... Suffice it only to declare that the Zionist Organization and the Government of Israel — which are indeed very real and active — are none other than the centre of the "Elders of Zion" who continue to hatch their plans. (Translated from the Hebrew.)

It has recently been suggested that Israel should seriously probe the reasons why anti-Zionism has repaced antisemitism. The answer, as far as I am concerned, is that we could not be more uninterested. Why Israel is and continues to be the object of so much venom is a story as old as Israel itself and certainly dates back to the day Israel made its covenant with God — which is probably the key element in this historical puzzle. Beyond that we really could not care less. It would in any event take far too long for us to psychoanalyse all of our tormentors and detractors and the findings will not add much to what we already know.

Is it really any wonder that there is no delirium in Israel

today and that the mood is that of sobriety and caution? And yet that is not all we feel these days. For as we combine to project this air of reserve there is in the heart of every one of us a deep feeling of great and profound hope. Rejoice, O Israel, for peace may yet come to thy tents! And when it comes Israel will neither forget its detractors nor fail to remember its friends.

5

European Attitudes to the Peace Process

Europe and Arab-Israeli Peacemaking
A Critique

The Twenty-Second Selig Brodetsky Memorial Lecture
The University of Leeds, May 18, 1982

For close to a year now the EEC has been engaged in a vigorous effort aimed at producing a formula to resolve one of the most complex and intractable issues of our time, namely the Arab-Israel dispute. In taking upon itself this onerous task Europe has been claiming title to an impressive list of credentials which — in its eyes at least — qualify and justify it in assuming such a heavy responsibility. These include some if not all of the following:

1. *Impartiality.* Europe is poised, so to speak, half-way between the two poles of the Arab-Israeli controversy and possesses a fair and impartial position on the issues in dispute.

2. *Respect for Camp David.* Far from contravening or competing with the Camp David peace process, Europe's efforts are designed to be complementary and supportive of it.

3. *Honest Brokerage.* All that Europe seeks to achieve is a judicious formula for a negotiated settlement by the parties themselves. No imposition is envisaged or entertained. It is for the parties to accept or to reject

* Reprinted with permission from *The University of Leeds Review 1981.*

Europe's formula or, better still, to compromise and to agree upon it.

4. *Legitimate Interests.* Europe's interest in the matter is at one and the same time its own vital stake in the stabilisation of the Middle East — the strategic and economic cockpit of our time — and the peace and well-being of the Middle East and of the countries directly involved.

5. *Expertise.* Given its historic involvement in and veteran knowledge of the affairs of the region, Europe commands a fund of expertise and statesmanship which uniquely equip it for the purpose of discharging a Middle East peacemaking mission.

As the party likely to be most immediately affected by the success or failure — or the mere exercise — of Europe's present Middle Eastern enterprise, an Israeli comment on these European claims may not be out of place.

1. *Europe's Impartiality.* Europe's present gospel on the Middle East — at least until amended or superseded by another — is the Venice Declaration by European Heads of State of June 1980. An analysis of the Venice Declaration should therefore provide a reasonably accurate indication of Europe's balance or imbalance.

With the exception of the introductory and concluding paragraphs every single one of the Declaration's eleven points is attuned and adapted to the Arab position:

Point Two of the Venice Declaration affirms Europe's obligation "...to play a special role and... to work in a more concrete way towards peace". Since 1973 Israel has consistently opposed an active European role in Middle East peacemaking in view of Europe's growing subservience to Arab economic blackmail, be it related to Europe's energy requirements, markets for its products or investment in its money markets. This subservience has been painfully clear since the traumatic days of the Yom Kippur War when not one European country was willing to make available its facilities to American supply planes on their way to an embattled Israel — the victim of the most flagrant act of aggression in recent years. In one notable instance a prominent European country also refused to supply Israel with spare parts for Centurion tanks purchased in years past.

Point Three endorses the historic resolutions 242 and 338 and then proceeds to nullify this endorsement by linking it to declarations of the EEC in the years 1977, 1978 and 1979 which constitute milestones in the EEC's systematic and progressive disengagement from the principles of Resolutions 242 and 338.

Point Four includes the only concession to an Israeli "viewpoint", namely Israel's right to exist for which Israel is eternally grateful and which it is happy to reciprocate by recognising the right to exist of every one of the ten members of the European Economic Community. However, unlike Israel's unconditional recognition of the European countries' right to exist, the Community in its Venice Declaration suggests the juxtaposition of Israel's right to national existence and security against that of a party whose prospective leadership — according to the European scheme of things — predicated its national claims and aspirations on their very denial to Israel.

Point Five raises the spectre of an Israel reduced to dependence for its physical survival on international guarantees such as have proven totally irrelevant and ineffective so many times in the past, in the Middle East and elsewhere.

171

Point Six invokes the terminology of "self-determination" for the Palestinians, which is a mere code word for an independent Palestinian state.

Point Seven calls for the association of the Palestine Liberation Organization (PLO) in the negotiations thus providing a clue as to who according to the EEC is expected to provide the leadership for the envisaged Palestinian state.

Point Eight offers advance notice of intentions to undo the unity of Jerusalem as the eternal capital of Israel.

Point Nine makes a mockery of the Community's reference to Resolution 242 by providing a broad hint as to the fullness of the withdrawal which is expected of Israel, though the Resolution specifically and deliberately refrains from any mention of complete withdrawal from territories occupied since 1967. This is what Lord George Brown — who was Foreign Secretary at the time — has to say on the meaning and intent of Resolution 242:

> It (the Resolution) does *not* call for Israeli withdrawal from "the" territories recently occupied, nor does it use the word "all". It would have been impossible to get the resolution through if either of these words had been included, but it does set out the lines on which negotiations for a settlement must take place. Each side must be prepared to give up something: the resolution doesn't attempt to say *precisely* what, because that is what negotiations for a peace treaty must be about.*

Point Nine also includes a reference to the gravest peril to international peace since Attila the Hun, namely the

* George Brown, *In My Way,* London, Victor Gollancz, 1971, p. 233.

172

twenty-thousand-odd Israelis who have settled in the Golan, the West Bank and the Gaza Strip in the past fourteen years.

So much for Europe's impartiality.

2. *European Respect for the Camp David Agreements.* The most telling aspect of the Venice Declaration is the absence from it of any mention of the Camp David agreements and the relegation of the historic Egyptian-Israeli Peace Treaty to mere "agreements (with a small "a") signed between Egypt and Israel". It is not without good reason that the "European Initiative" has been described by a prominent European statesman as giving encouragement to "friendly Arab states who felt bound for their own reasons to stand aside from the Camp David process".

A comparative analysis of the Camp David agreements and the principles of the Venice Declaration clearly bears out the sharp inconsistencies between the two approaches.

a. Resolution 242 which is the linchpin of the Camp David agreements has to all intents and purposes been jettisoned by the European Community. No amount of lip service to the Resolution can make up for the complete disregard for its basic principles.

b. While Camp David stipulated that negotiations between Israel and its neighbours should be free of dictate or predetermined prescriptions, Europe seeks not only to establish a precise prescription for a settlement but also contemplates its imposition.

c. According to Camp David Israel is to be a full partner — along with Egypt, Jordan and representatives of the Palestinian people — in determining the future of Judea, Samaria and Gaza. There is to be no change or transformation in the status of these territories except with Israel's

173

full agreement. According to Europe's own interpretation of the Venice Declaration Israelis have hardly any part or say in determining the future of the territories.

d. Camp David specifically and purposely refrained from any reference to "self-determination". What it did was to establish for the first time — and after considerable compromise and concessions — a measured process and framework whereby a solution is to be sought for the problem of the Palestinian Arabs. True to its disregard for the Camp David agreements the Venice Declaration arbitrarily substitutes the slogan and code word of "self-determination" for what was perhaps the genius of the Camp David agreements, namely time and open-mindedness.

e. Nowhere in Camp David is Jerusalem mentioned and for good reason. The Venice Declaration confers upon Jerusalem the very prominence and centrality which for the sake of all concerned should be studiously avoided.

f. Camp David does not refer to nor proscribe Jewish settlement in Judea, Samaria and Gaza. The Venice Declaration declares these to be "serious obstacles to peace" carefully omitting to mention such "minor" obstacles to peace as the "Palestinian Covenant" which calls for no less than the elimination of the State of Israel.

g. According to Camp David Israel's eastern border is to be determined through negotiations between Israel and Jordan. In endorsing the principle of self-determination the Venice Declaration invests the responsibility for determining the future of the territories of Judea, Samaria and Gaza exclusively in the hands of the Palestinians and thus also ignores the critical strategic importance of this border to Israel's security.

174

h. The Camp David agreements call for the establishment of autonomy in Judea, Samaria and Gaza for a period of five years, leaving all options open beyond that. The Venice Declaration effectively closes every option bar one, namely the laying of the foundations for an independent Palestinian state though it knows this to be anathema to all sane Israelis for the fearful danger it represents to them.

i. The Camp David agreements call for the partial withdrawal of Israeli forces in Judea, Samaria and Gaza and their redeployment in accordance with Israel's security needs. The Venice Declaration seeks the establishment of the principle of total Israeli withdrawal.

j. The Camp David agreements make reference to the need for special arrangements for Palestinian Arabs displaced as a result of the 1967 war and to the 1948 refugees while making a very clear distinction between these two categories. The Venice Declaration substitutes "peoplehood" for "refugees", opening a veritable Pandora's box.

k. The Camp David agreements are predicated on continued and pivotal American participation in the peace process. The Venice Declaration is the clarion call of an independent so-called "European initiative".

l. The Camp David agreements not only welcome but urge the participation of Palestinian Arabs — residents of Judea, Samaria and Gaza — in the resolution of their problem and most emphatically do not envisage or allow for the involvement of the PLO in this process in any way, shape or form. The Venice Declaration no less than seeks to introduce into the peace process this nihilistic element which is sworn by word and deed to the obstruction and destruction of any and all peaceful solutions.

175

It is entirely permissible for any party to dissociate itself from the Camp David agreements. One cannot, however, have one's cake and eat it too, embark on a course that is clearly in conflict with the Camp David agreements and at the same time claim fidelity to them.

3. *Europe's Honest Brokerage.* Europe's next port of call after Venice was Luxembourg where the EEC "approved the decision of the Ministers of Foreign Affairs to undertake consideration of the matter with the aim of clarifying and giving substance to the Venice principles. That consideration [had] resulted in the drafting of a report on the principal problems relating to a comprehensive settlement under the following headings: withdrawal, self-determination, security in the Middle East, Jerusalem." In other words not content with the enunciation of a list of principles, Europe now undertook — through the instrumentality of four of its respective governments — to draw up specific proposals relating to all the principal issues of the Arab-Israel dispute.

Nothing has been made officially known of the details of these proposals which have been kept a very close secret. All we have been told is that papers were drafted and submitted to the European Council and then adopted by it as representing a European consensus on the details of a Middle East settlement. Enough, however, has been leaked or otherwise revealed to give good cause and ground for the suspicion that the Venice Declaration was merely the tip of an iceberg whose submerged mass is the "Luxembourg Papers". Moreover from what we know about this submerged mass there is ample reason to fear that if ever it were to make contact with the process of Arab-Israeli peacemaking it would have the same effect on

176

it as that submerged mass which brought down the *Titanic*.

Following are some of the main points in the "Luxembourg Papers" as reported by *Le Soir* of Brussels on December 28–29, 1980. This report has never been authoritatively denied by the EEC.

"1. *Israeli Withdrawal.* According to the Nine, the withdrawal of Israeli forces, as stated by Security Council Resolution 242 must be complete and concern all the territories occupied in June 1967, the West Bank, Gaza, East Jerusalem and the Golan. The withdrawal should take effect within a maximum period of 2 years.

"As for the Israeli settlements which are regarded as illegal, they will have to be dismantled" with the possible exception of "those which existed in the West Bank before the conflict of May 1948." The latter would be maintained and their inhabitants would live there from now on as foreigners.

"2. *Self-Determination of the Palestinians.* Self-determination would give the West Bank and Gaza a choice of three options:

1. An independent Palestinian state
2. A federation with Jordan
3. A federation with Jordan and Israel.

"A referendum organised during a period of transition, will be supervised by an elected Advisory Committee. All the Palestinians will have the right to vote with special preference given to the inhabitants of the occupied territories (about 1.2 million out of a population of about 4 million Palestinians).

"3. *Security and Guarantees.* The Venice Declaration stated that the guarantees of a peace settlement should be provided by the UN following a decision of the Security

Council, and should the occasion arise, on the basis of other procedures, mutually agreed. It was said then that the Nine were ready to take part in a system of international guarantees, concrete and binding, including on the ground. The document (i.e. The Luxembourg Papers), takes up those ideas again and asserts that the guarantees should apply to all the sides.

"An international force of the United Nations, with European participation, could be called for missions of control and observation in the demilitarized areas.

"On a larger scale the Nine also suggest a reduction of military forces (in terms of armaments and of troops).

"4. *Options for Jerusalem.* Regarding Jerusalem, the Nine consider, in accordance with UN resolutions, that all that has been done since the partition of Palestine on November 27, 1947 is illegal. Therefore they propose several solutions:

— Return to the International Status (The Corpus Separatum) as stated by the Partition Resolution of 1947.

— Division of the city, placing the holy sites under religious authority.

— Division of the city, making the Old City an international place.

"In the case of the division of the city, the latter could be placed under a joint administration.

"5. *Return of the Refugees.* Concerning the issue of the Palestinian refugees, their return to the territories evacuated by Israel should be done according to ways to be determined.

"For the rest, the resolution of the UN General Assembly of December 11, 1949, still upholds the right of the refugees to return to their homes or to compensation for their property and belongings."

If such is the detailed nature and scope of the EEC's "Luxembourg Papers" then it is difficult to accept the EEC's protestations that what it is embarked upon is a mere laying down of general principles for Arab-Israeli settlement and not the formulation of a comprehensive plan which in view of Israel's clear opposition to its concepts could — in theory at least — only be imposed on it through the application of massive pressure.

That this may well be the case is suggested by the manner in which the EEC has refrained from any consultation with the party most likely to be affected by its efforts, namely Israel. At no time did the EEC consult with Israel about its prospective ideas for the settlement of the Arab-Israel conflict although Israel makes up at least 50 per cent of that conflict. This in itself seems to suggest that the EEC, which must be aware of the effect of its partiality and aloofness on Israel's trust in its motives and objectives, is hardly thinking in terms of friendly European persuasion. What seems more likely is that it may be contemplating the employment of the services of another party which does indeed enjoy Israel's trust and confidence and also has considerable leverage over it as befits a country which has done so much for Israel's well-being and security as the United States. Whether or not the United States will or will not be amenable to European proddings to apply this leverage over Israel is at the very least debatable, for American *raisons d'état*. Whatever the case it should be understood that any European efforts to induce the United States to adopt the EEC position and to work towards its enforcement upon Israel will not fall far short of unaccept-

179

able interference in the relations between two friendly
countries, and in this instance between two *very* friendly
countries.

4. *Protection of legitimate interests.*

It has been argued that Europe has the right to pursue
any policy which it considers consonant with its interests.
This is readily conceded as perfectly legitimate just as is the
complementary claim that it is for Europe to determine
where its interests lie. At the same time, as the party most
likely to be affected by Europe's exercise of these very
legitimate rights, Israel is entitled to express an opinion on
the matter.

There are in theory two possible scenarios. The first is
that Europe will have its way: Israel will be forced to
withdraw to the 1967 lines. Jerusalem will be redivided in
one way or another. A Palestinian state will be established
in the areas evacuated and masses of Palestinians will
exercise their right to return and in effect to inundate both
the territories evacuated and Israel proper. Such a scenario
can only spell one result: the complete emasculation of
Israel and its subsequent disintegration under a massive
Arab onslaught either in stages or outright. And no combination of international guarantees and UN peacekeeping
forces could possibly make any material difference in such
circumstances. It is in any event very unlikely that a
Europe which has not been able to resist Arab pressure
until now, will do so in a situation which will call not just
for political exertions but for the commitment of massive
military force, i.e., going to war with the Arabs for Israel
— time permitting of course! Can anyone really visualize
European countries dispatching planeloads of troops to a
beleaguered and surrounded Israel desperately fighting for

its life when serious doubts exist in Europe *today* as to whether it has the means or the will to participate in an American-inspired rapid deployment force designed to protect *Europe's* vital oil supplies from the Middle East?

The other scenario — and much the likelier one — is that Israel will resist with every ounce of its not-insignificant energy any attempt to impose upon it a European-style settlement. Small and harassed though it may be, Israel possesses very substantial power and resilience as well as unbounded will and determination to survive. Those who contemplate imposition in the furtherance of their interests should have no illusions about Israel's willingness and ability to commit all of its resources to protect its *own* most vital interests.

While Israel has the wherewithal to resist effectively and successfully any attempt to coerce it to act against its will and interests, this is hardly a scenario relished by Israelis because it can only spell tensions and dangers resulting from the country's further isolation and the consequent blow to its credibility in the eyes of its enemies. An isolated Israel is a prospect that should not be relished by anyone who has a true interest in and concern for Middle East peace. Israel's enemies too should reject such a prospect!

Lest there be any illusions about the magnitude of an all-out conflict in the Middle East resulting from either scenario, stock should be taken of the immense accumulation of arms and armaments in the Middle East and especially in the hands of Israel's enemies. Following are some figures on this subject.

The Arab States excluding Egypt can today field the following force in a war against Israel:

1,214,500 men; 2,443 advanced war planes; 13,534

tanks; 10,945 armoured personnel carriers; 9,027 artillery pieces. These figures are better understood and appreciated when compared with some NATO figures. According to the Institute for Strategic Studies, NATO's forces along its norther and central fronts include:

626,000 men (as against twice as many Arab troops)

7,000 tanks (half the combined Arab force)

1,900 war planes (a third less than the Arabs possess).

The force that Israel is able to field against this vast concentration of planes, tanks, guns and men can never be more than a fraction of it, given Israel's numerical inferiority and meagre resources. This notwithstanding, an all-out Arab-Israeli war will see the greatest tank battles, artillery duels, missile exchanges and aerial combat in the entire history of warfare. But this is not all, for the arms race continues unabated.

According to the Stockholm International Peace Research Institute, Middle Eastern military spending is running at more than 40 billion dollars a year out of a world total of 500 billion dollars. In fact the Arab world today possesses the largest arsenal of arms in the world after the USA and the USSR — far exceeding that of Europe.

The biggest arms customer in the Arab world, or anywhere else outside the superpowers, is Saudi Arabia which spent on arms and military installations no less than 27 billion dollars last year alone. This spending spree continues to escalate and not a week goes by without a distinguished statesman announcing with great satisfaction the conclusion of yet another arms deal with Saudi Arabia and any number of Arab states.

Europe will of course reject the idea that it could possibly be seeking the realisation of either of these scenarios and will in return brandish its own much-heralded "comprehensive settlement". In practice, however, the chances for an instantaneous "comprehensive settlement" of the sort which Europe advocated for the Middle East are about as good as they are anywhere else, namely nil. The continued pursuit of a European-style settlement — let alone its realisation — can only lead to grievous damage either to Israel's capacity to defend itself — which Israel considers the only sure way of guaranteeing its security and survival — or to its credibility in the eyes of its foes and its trust in the support and understanding of its friends. The consequences in both cases can only spell disaster for the entire Middle East and for all who today openly claim critical dependence on it. Could this possibly be in Europe's interest?

5. *Expertise*. Europe's present Middle East policy and practices raise many questions. Here are some which have occurred to Israelis at least:

A.   What is one to make of a policy which chooses to denigrate the first successful peace process in the history of the modern Middle East? Those who make short shrift of the first Arab-Israeli peace should also realise that in so doing they are causing no small number of Israelis to ponder the wisdom of having invested so much in it and run such enormous risks for it.

B.   How does one rate a policy which ignores the most vital — indeed existential — interests of one party to the Arab-Israeli dispute?

C.   What could be the wisdom of deliberately and systematically excluding Israel from any genuine dialogue about matters affecting Israel's peace, well-being and security?

183

D. What could be the purpose of a policy which is almost calculated to ensure that the party most directly affected by it should cease to have any confidence and trust in the motives and objectives of those who pursue it? To spurn historic relationships and traditions of common enterprise is to cause serious damage to the fabric of genuine bonds of amity and high regard. What possible interest could be served by that?

E. What is one to make of a policy which if ever it were to be realised is bound to plunge the Middle East into frightful conflict primarily because of its disregard for the views, opinions, fears, suspicions *and* most vital interests of the country most likely to pay the price for its failings?

F. Has anyone stopped to consider the implications and consequences of a policy which actively and knowingly seeks to embrace the head of the octopus of international terror whose tentacles today reach everywhere and everyone and for whom nothing is sacred and no one exempt?

G. What does one say of a policy which claims to seek lasting and secure peace for the peoples of the Middle East while at the same time putting in their hands unlimited quantities of the most lethal weapons and armaments? All this without serious consideration for its impact on the fragile societies involved, the tenuous military balances affected and the fate of the party most likely to serve as a target for all these weapons if and when — as is the fate of all weapons — they are to be used. Those who think that such things as a tenuous military balance can be freely tampered with should take note of the present tensions in the Middle East and remind themselves how low the threshold of war in the area still is. As they do so, they might

184

also wish to reconsider the wisdom of inevitably obliging Israel to adjust its strategic priorities as certain parties which had best be kept on the fringes of the Arab-Israel conflict are converted through the massive infusion of arms into very formidable adversaries.

Admittedly these questions are today being raised mostly by Israelis. Nonetheless Europeans too would do well to ponder them.

The Peace with Egypt

Speech at
"Conservative Friends of Israel" Luncheon
Conservative Party Conference
Brighton, October 11, 1979

Thank you, Mr. Chairman, for your kind words of welcome and for your warm expression of friendship for my country. Thank you, ladies and gentlemen, for joining in this gathering which, with your permission, I shall register as an act of friendship for Israel.

Past history and present circumstances have developed in our people a special sensitivity to matters of friendship. We are a people upon which friendship has not been lavished in centuries past, and it is not readily available in these times either. In over four thousand years of national existence, we have experienced more isolation and loneliness than friendship. Other peoples have also known isolation. It was not so long ago when this country stood alone.

A great leader of yours, Winston Churchill, who was also a devoted friend of Zionism — summed it up in a volume entitled *Alone*. The difference is that in our case it has not been a matter of one volume, but of an endless series of volumes on the same theme.

I shall not embark on a detailed history of the people of Israel, but I shall dwell for a minute on the subject of friendship for Israel in *these* times, not so much on its moral abstractions as on its practical applications.

186

The people of Israel are today engaged in an exacting national effort, involving both deep soul-searching and realistic stock-taking. The issue is peace, but at issue is survival. To believe our detractors — and they are legion and voluble — Israel is disposed to give very little for peace. This is unfair. It not only disregards the entire meaning and character of Israel, but also the substantial concessions we have made and enormous risks we have recently taken in the pursuit of peace with Egypt.

Let me cite some of these concessions and sacrifices, whose magnitude and significance has been dimmed by a constant barrage of criticism of Israeli policies.

The Sinai Peninsula in its entirety, that strategic depth which was our salvation six years ago, is to be given up.

Sharm-el-Sheikh, the flashpoint of two wars and the gateway to Israel's southern approaches, is to be handed back.

The Rafiah Salient — which was to have provided us with a strategic wedge on that classic invasion route into Israel, the Roman Via Maris, is being forfeited.

We are abandoning a network of no less than five air-fields including two which have been described as the most modern and sophisticated between the Mediterranean and the Pacific. This will seriously limit the manoeuvrability of Israel's air force, the mainstay of our national defence. All in all we are giving up a logistical infrastructure valued at upwards of four billion pounds sterling.

In addition, we are returning to Egypt oil fields, yielding a substantial part of Israel's fuel requirements, and worth thirty-seven dollars a barrel on today's spot market. This places us in a serious predicament as far as oil supplies are concerned. I might add that we have so far met with disappointing responses in our efforts to recoup this self-inflicted shortfall elsewhere.

Apparently, only superpowers may claim the right to strategic depth, to airfields and military installations deployed in other people's national territories, and to the right to be sensitive to the appearance of a handful of troops off their shores. These are not Israel's prerogative.

We gave up all this in return for peace. We do not complain about the price. All we ask is that due note be taken of Israel's contribution to the making of that peace, and the enormous risks we have incurred by doing so. For that peace that we have signed with Egypt is still not a comprehensive peace embracing all Israel's neighbours, though it is undoubtedly the first and most important building block in the eventual comprehensive peace that *we* seek. The rest of the Arab world continues to bristle with ever more arms and ever more threats. There are no less than five thousand tanks on our eastern flank. Those are soon to be reinforced with two hundred more of the finest tanks money can buy.

In spite of the magnitude of our sacrifice in the search for peace with our neighbours, the image dubbed on us today is that of "intransigence", "obstructionism" and downright "warmongering", and this at the very time when we are engaged in an effort aimed at untangling one of the most complex issues in the Arab-Israeli conflict. Instead of encouragement and understanding, we are subjected to criticism and censure; in place of being granted the smallest measure of patience and trust, we are pushed and cajoled.

Is this the way to help a small, beleaguered and threatened country appraise its national priorities and essential strategic requirements? Is this the way to instill in a perennially betrayed nation a measure of minimal trust and confidence in order to ease its crushing burden of decision-making? Above all, is all this likely to advance the cause of peace? Hardly.

It would behoove all those who contribute in one way or another to these pressures to ponder whether in so doing they may not overreach and compromise the miraculous progress achieved so far, thereby jeopardising the substantial regional — I repeat regional — stability that has been made possible by the Egyptian-Israeli peace. When the two most powerful states in any region make peace between them, they thereby generate a substantial element of regional stability. It is *this* achievement which should be noted and heeded, and not the crowing and protestations of the rejectionists and the assassins.

Let no one belittle the immense strategic importance of the Egyptian-Israeli peace. Let no one denigrate *any* peace in the Middle East, no matter how big or how small. Let no one begrudge Egypt and Israel their peace, whatever its scope and dimensions. Those who fought in all of the five Arab-Israeli wars have had their Passchendaeles and Sommes. We do not need another regional conflagration in order to conclude, as the Europeans finally did, that war is not a viable option. Our leaders have already declared and vowed "No more war". There is no reason why they should not be believed: Everyone who has a stake in Middle East peace — as everybody has today — should shudder at the thought of a collapse of the important measure of stability achieved by the Egyptian-Israeli peace. The cost and the consequences of such a collapse are too grim to consider.

Hence the importance of friendship for an Israel engaged in the effort to consolidate the peace, and if at all possible to expand it. Hence the value of every expression of understanding for Israel's predicament as we pursue this effort. Hence the need for recognition of the limits of our country's potential for risk and sacrifice. Hence the importance of Conservative Friends of Israel, Labour Friends of Israel, Liberal Friends of Israel — British Friends of Israel.

Mr. Chairman, ladies and gentlemen, this country was with us when we embarked on one of the most dramatic chapters in the realisation of Zionism — the Jewish people's national liberation movement and the oldest national liberation movement in recorded history. May I humbly submit that it would be most fitting if you stayed with us as we proceed to consummate our national struggle through the fulfilment of the most fervent of our dreams — making peace with our neighbours. Thank you.

190

What Price Peace?

Speech to the Anglo-Israel Association
Annual General Meeting
London, December 13, 1979

In March of this year, Abba Eban, Member of Knesset and former Foreign Minister of Israel, came over to speak to you, directly after having participated in the historic debate and vote on the Egyptian-Israeli Peace Treaty in the Knesset in Jerusalem.

In his inimitable way, Mr. Eban then gave expression to the wide range of emotions, sentiments and feelings experienced by all who participated in that historic parliamentary session. It was an address brimming with hope and confidence, but at the same time, also a sober assessment of the distance yet to be covered, and especially the challenge of the next round of negotiations with its pitfalls and inevitable difficulties.

Cautious though he was, neither Mr. Eban nor you ladies and gentlemen who listened to him that night, nor for that matter any sober or sane person anywhere, could possibly have imagined or dreamt that within nine months that same treaty would be condemned by the United Nations General Assembly. Who could possibly have believed then, or for that matter now, that this almost miraculous breakthrough which we continue most firmly to believe is the beginning of a new era in the history of the Middle East — the dawn of peace between Arab and

191

Israeli — could be the subject of condemnation by a world body conceived as the custodian of world peace?

This was not the only vote of censure passed in the United Nations session which has now, fortunately, drawn to a close. There were at least 40 more resolutions passed this year condemning Israel for every conceivable and inconceivable crime as every possible abuse continued to be poured over the State of Israel culminating once again in the equation of Zionism with racism.

How does one account for that? What could we possibly have done to deserve all this? To be meted out such punishment? It most certainly could not be in retribution for having, say, failed to live up to any of our commitments under the Egyptian-Israeli peace treaty nor any other part of the Camp David agreements. Since signing and ratifying the treaty, Israel has performed impeccably: It has evacuated all those parts of Sinai which it was committed to do, and which already amount to two thirds of the Peninsula. Barren and empty though it is, the Sinai Desert has been of the greatest strategic importance to Israel. It was into this desert that we could withdraw in 1973 when suddenly pounced upon, and when every available resource had to be diverted to the Northern Front where the pressure was most acute. And who knows how it might all have ended had we not had that desert into which to pull back, instead of into the populated regions of southern Israel, with its exposed and congested system of communications so vital to Israel's ability to muster its reserves which are the bulk of its armed forces?

Soon it will be the turn of yet more chunks of Sinai to be handed over until eventually the entire Peninsula will have been returned to the Egyptians along with some of Israel's most advanced airfields, its naval and air base in Sharm-el-Sheikh, and across the Peninsula that cluster of Jewish settlements known as the Rafiah Salient, which will now have to be plucked out of the desert which they had converted into flowering gardens. In evacuating Sinai, Israel will therefore be divesting itself not only of the strategic depth afforded by it, but of a great deal more including:

1. A very significant part of its capacity to deploy and operate its air force — the mainstay of its defence and the equivalent of what in other countries consists of fleets of B-52's, Polaris submarines together with ICBM's and early-warning systems, not to speak of protective umbrellas for civilian populations and air cover for ground forces.

2. The gateway to Israel's southern approaches and its outlet to the continents of Africa, Asia and Australasia. In years past, the closure of this gateway was twice the cause of major wars in the Middle East.

3. A strategic wedge consisting of Israeli civilian and military presence at the point of entry from the northern Sinai into the Gaza Strip which was meant to serve as a trip-wire across the path of any would-be invader coming up that classic invasion route known as the Via Maris.

That is not all that we are leaving behind in Sinai. In accordance with our obligations we have also given up oil — a commodity whose economic and strategic worth does not require any elaboration.

A few weeks ago, Israel gave up an oil field which, when we handed it over to the Egyptians, was producing the equivalent of almost 30% of Israel's energy needs, and which in two or three years from now could have been developed to supply Israel with all of its energy needs. All this at a time when Israel no longer has access to its traditional oil supplies and when the price of an oil barrel on the spot market in Rotterdam is 40 dollars today, promising to be 50 dollars within a year from now. All this on the eve of an era when nations may well go to war against each other for possession of or access to oil.

It is our fervent hope and prayer, sustained now by a formal peace treaty with Egypt, that never again shall we be confronted with a situation in which the availability of air and sea bases and of strategic wedges and trip-wires will suddenly assume critical importance. And yet who can or will guarantee that such an eventuality will never again arise? This in any event is the extent to which we have committed ourselves under the Egyptian-Israeli peace treaty and this is the measure in which we have been true to our commitments. And for this we are today condemned in the United Nations General Assembly, at Third World gatherings and regrettably at other forums as well.

Or could it be that such is our lot because of Israel's failure to address itself to that complex and highly charged issue of the Palestinian Arabs? But surely we are innocent of that charge too: Under the Camp David agreements, Israel accepted some very clear obligations in this regard, and it is this very same list of obligations which we are these days actively, earnestly and genuinely engaged in honouring. Given the vast distortions created by allegations to the contrary, let me repeat the key ones:

"...Israel and Egypt set themselves the goal of completing the negotiations within one year — begun between them one month after the ratification of the Egyptian-Israeli peace treaty and aimed at reaching agreement on "transitional arrangements for the West Bank and Gaza for a period not exceeding five years. In order to provide full autonomy to the inhabitants under these arrangements, the Israeli military govenment and its civilian administration will be withdrawn as soon as a self-governing authority has been freely elected by the inhabitants of these areas to replace the existing military government.... These new arrangements should give due consideration to both the principle of self-government... and to the legitimate security concerns of the parties involved."

"...When the self-governing authority (administrative council) in the West Bank and Gaza is established and inaugurated, the transitional period of five years will begin" as soon as possible, but not later than the third year after the beginning of the transitional period. "Negotiations will take place (among Egypt, Israel, Jordan and representatives of the West Bank and Gaza) to determine the final status of the West Bank and Gaza and its relationship with its neighbours and to conclude a peace treaty between Israel and Jordan by the end of the transitional period."

This is what Israel has committed itself to do and this is what we are presently earnestly trying to do. And yet it is as if all of this: all the concessions, all of the risks, all of the commitments, have never been contracted for nor respected by us. Such is the chorus of censure and condemnation to which Israel is being subjected today, and such are some of the ideas and notions being given apparently increasing credence today, not only in the United Nations in New York where one has come to expect any aberration, but also elsewhere, where one has the right to hope for more sanity and fairness.

Here is what the leader writer on Middle East issues of a distinguished London newspaper has written as part of a call to the West no less than to re-evaluate its attitude towards President Sadat's peace efforts: "There is virtual consensus that the Camp David framework does not provide for an adequate basis for a general Arab-Israeli peace. Such a peace requires a solution of the Palestinian problem, and no solution of the Palestinian problem could be accepted as valid by the great majority of Palestinians or by other Arab states, unless the PLO were involved in it.... The PLO... does not, it is true, recognise the right of the State of Israel to exist, and perhaps is not likely to in the forseeable future. To expect Palestinians to accept the appropriation of their country for a Jewish state is comparable to expecting Germans to accept the forcible divisions of their country as right. They do not and they will not." Just like the Germans, "if given a state of their own in part of Palestine, the Palestinians would thereafter seek to re-unite the country by 'peaceful and democratic means'." "We must use democratic means", our leader writer quotes his PLO interlocutor as saying, "because the aim is democratic. The Jews have to be persuaded, not forced, to abandon racist Zionism and join with the Arabs in a democratic state."

Absurd as may be the thoughts and ideas which our leader writer has been propagating they are nonetheless disturbing, for they are also a sign of the times. A sign of the growing inclination to yield to blackmail, to accept the easy palliative and to settle for the most expedient. No wonder the entire Western World finds itself today dangling at the end of a string of oil tankers constantly threatening to snap, and no wonder that as a result the West faces one of its most critical dilemmas in many years.

At stake today is not only the West's ability to maintain its economic viability but also its social fabric and its moral and ethical standards. Such is the challenge facing the West today in the Middle East. Hardly at its *Western* end i.e. in the Arab-Israeli arena, but rather eastwards along both sides of the Persian Gulf, southwards to Aden, and across the Horn of Africa. And yet, with the notable exception of the events surrounding the hijacking of an entire western Embassy, it is not this historic challenge which is attracting the attention of the media and the public, and apparently also of governments. Rather it is the old Arab-Israeli conflict which continues to preoccupy people most. As if there was no peace treaty between Israel and Egypt, as if the Arab-Israeli conflict had not been defused to a very large degree by this same treaty; as if the threat of another Arab-Israeli war had not been considerably diminished by the commitment to peace on the part of the two countries which alone in the Middle East have participated in all five previous Arab-Israeli wars.

One would have thought that peace between Israel and Egypt after no less than thirty years of conflict would give rise to some optimism and satisfaction. Enough to enable people to address themselves to other much more pressing issues and inflammable situations of much greater strategic and economic importance to the Western World, such as the ones presently unfolding in an area roughly within a radius of 1,000 kilometres from Aden.

We do not ask for accolades for having made peace with Egypt. We do not ask for recompense for the sacrifices we have made in order to make that peace possible. And neither do we seek guarantees in the event that the risks we have undertaken ever prove to have been unwarranted. All we ask is: firstly for a sober assessment of the truly remarkable geopolitical significance of the fact that Israel and Egypt have signed a peace treaty and are gradually moving towards the realisation of this peace in concrete and practical terms. Secondly, for the Egyptian-Israeli peace treaty to be recognised for what it is, namely, not some minor step involving Israel and one of the host of Arab countries with which it has been at war, but rather one which involves the two most important components of the Arab-Israeli conflict, and therefore constituting a very major and indispensible development without which there can be no progress towards that much-hailed comprehensive settlement. Thirdly, that this peace which Israel has made with Egypt be regarded as one with which neither Egypt nor Israel are content to rest.

This is no separate peace that we have made with Egypt, but very much a part of the ongoing effort to which we have committed ourselves. An effort which is presently being extended to include the very complex issue of the Palestinian Arabs living in Judea, Samaria and Gaza.

The goal we have set ourselves is attainable once people concede that there are problems which, because of their special constraints and circumstances, defy the pat "here-and-now" type of solution, but rather call for the creation of new realities and new relationships centred on the elemental need to coexist peacefully within the confines of a small and congested area into which history and fate have crowded them.

In this respect the problem we are talking about is hardly unique these days, and as in similar dilemmas the only possible approach is one which seeks to focus on the

198

common need to provide people with security from war and want, rather than on national, religious, or ethnic confrontation.

As to the geopolitical wisdom of substituting a Palestinian-Israeli confrontation for Egyptian-Israeli peacemaking, which is apparently what our aforementioned leader writer seems to recommend, let me say that there can be no better prescription for unprecedented disaster for all of our peoples. Moreover, such a calamity will hardly remain confined to our immediate area, but is bound to envelop the entire area with the most far-reaching consequences also for all those who have chosen to make their future almost totally dependent on energy supplies from it. Ironically, this is almost guaranteed by the vast arsenals that have been amassed in the Arab world as a result of the West's frantic efforts to recycle petrodollars for weapons, thus converting each and every Arab state in the area into a potential belligerent in any future Middle East war.

The Middle East is today the world's most volatile area. Our end of it, however, is the only part which offers hope when compared with the eruptions taking place elsewhere in the area. Where else in the Middle East is anyone engaged in peacemaking except in Israel and Egypt? Where else in the Middle East are people seeking to put an end to warfare and bloodshed, in order to herald a better era in which man can live free of the scourge of war? Where else in the Middle East are people so anxious to be able to divert their meagre resources to the reconstruction of war-weary economies? Where else are nations engaged in converting old battlefields into trade routes? Where else in the Middle East are people talking of pooling their resources

199

in order to join together in making the desert bloom?

This is the true measure of what we are presently trying to do together with our Egyptian neighbours. And that, I submit to you, is also a correct reading of the state of affairs at our end of the Middle East, when seen against the background of events elsewhere in the area.

Whatever the case, there is confidence in our hearts that the course upon which Israel and Egypt have embarked is one from which there really is no return, and from which neither of us wishes to return. The only way back is that very one which our leaders have sworn to discard, as both solemnly declared in Jerusalem and many times since: "No more war!" "Peace!"

6

Israel and Europe

The Choice Before Europe

Address at the
Diplomatic and Commonwealth Writers Association of Britain
London, June 15, 1981

Israel's diplomatic relations with the countries that constitute the European Economic Community date back to the establishment of the state in 1948. There were exceptions: it took seventeen years before Israel could brace itself to accept the need for full diplomatic relations with Germany; not until 1975 did Israel and Ireland normalise their relations — though for reasons best known to Ireland; resident missions have yet to be established in the capitals of the respective countries; while Britain waited two years before extending Israel full de jure recognition — a somewhat rare case in the history of Britain's relations with former colonial possessions. Today Greece has yet to fully normalise its relations with Israel and prospective-member Spain seems bent on entering the Community with its non-relations with the Jewish state intact. As if to suggest that the "Spirit of 1492" lingers on and to remind us yet again that present-day Israeli attitudes and sensitivities towards the continent of Europe cannot be divorced from the Jewish people's European experience.

The people of the State of Israel and the nations of Europe have been formally related for a mere thirty-three years. In reality, however, we have known each other since the beginning of recorded European history, which corresponds to almost half of Israel's recorded history. With the exception of a few notable and mutually highly rewarding chapters, the Jewish people's association with Europe has been a harrowing experience and we shall in all likelihood bear its scars for a long time to come. Whether we wish it or not this is the historical background for European-Israeli relations and it is immaterial whether the European side agrees. What matters is that for us Europe will always remain both the scene of a magnificent cultural, intellectual and scientific common enterprise and the site of some of the worst manifestations of Christian man's inhumanity to his Jewish brother.

According to Europe's own testimony the point of departure for any discussion of present-day European-Israeli relations is the so-called Venice Declaration. This we have been advised is the basis of Europe's position on Arab-Israeli peace. The contents of the Venice Declaration are clear: with the exception of the introductory and concluding paragraphs all of the Declaration's eleven points but one are adapted and attuned to the Arab position. The only one which includes a concession to an Israeli viewpoint is the one which inter alia establishes "the right to existence and to security of all of the states in the region including Israel". A strange point to make about a state that has been sovereign and independent for some thirty-three years and is no less vital and viable than any of its European counterparts and which in addition can claim a continuous national experience longer than any in Europe. Nonetheless we are duly appreciative, and in reciprocating this European gesture declare our unreserved recognition of the right to secure national existence

204

of every one of the ten members of the EEC including prospective-member Spain.

Other than this single accommodation of an Israeli position — albeit somewhat qualified by its juxtaposition against a call for "justice for all peoples which implies the recognition of the legitimate rights of the Palestinian people" — the Venice Declaration is essentially a European attempt to synchronize an ever lower common European position with a consistently low common Arab position. In its attempt to approximate the Arab consensus Europe has accepted the Arab position on practically every central issue of the Arab-Israel dispute including: withdrawal — which is to be complete and therefore in contravention of Resolution 242; guarantees — which are envisaged as a substitute for Israel's ability to defend itself; Jerusalem — which may become any one of many things other than the united capital of Israel; and the Palestinians — which are accorded the right to self-determination in the full knowledge of what this code word implies. Crowning it all is the injunction that the PLO "will have to be associated with the negotiations".

Being excluded from the Community's consultations on matters affecting none other than our own most vital interests, we are not privy to the Community's subsequent elaboration of the Venice principles. All we have been told is that this has taken the form of a series of pronouncements commonly known as the Luxembourg Papers and the subjects of which are "withdrawal", "boundaries and security arrangements" and "self-determination for the Palestinians". From what little we know, however, we are reasonably satisfied that the EEC's position on these critical matters is in conflict not just with the policies of any conceivable Government of Israel but with the widest possible national consensus of the people of Israel. No sane Israeli will accept or countenance a scheme of things which is tantamount to the emasculation of Israel and its conversion from a country able to defend itself by itself into an international ward dependent for its survival on the good graces of others. No sane Israeli will accept the division of Jerusalem. And no sane Israeli could possibly view with other than the most profound alarm the prospect of the establishment of a Palestinian state ruled by an entity publicly sworn to the eradication of the Israeli state.

Revealing as the contents of the Venice Declaration may be, the document is even more significant for its omissions. Try as you may you will find no mention in the Venice Declaration of the Camp David agreements. It is no less than remarkable that a statement on the principles and modalities for peacemaking in the Middle East should not have mentioned by name the most important single achievement in the Middle East's tormented quest for peace. In place of the Camp David agreements reference is made to "agreements signed between Egypt and Israel in March 1979". In so doing, Europe has done two things: It has relegated the first Arab-Israeli Peace Treaty — between Israel and no less than its former foremost adversary — into a minor affair of the order of a cease-fire or armistice agreement and made short shrift of the most imaginative and magnanimous offer ever made to the Palestinians by Israel or anyone else for that matter.

What is the nature of this offer which Israel has made to the Palestinians and which Europe has not seen fit to mention in its manifesto on the Middle East for fear, one suspects, of running afoul of Camp David's "rejection-

206

ists"? "Old hat" as they may seem to some, here are its highlights as recorded in the Camp David agreements and as adopted by Israel and Egypt and attested by the United States.

    a. *Objectives.* "The Resolution of the Palestinian problem in all its aspects".

    b. *Principles.* "The negotiations shall be based on all the provisions and principles of UN Security Council Resolution 242...."

    "The solution from the negotiations must also recognise the legitimate rights of the Palestinian people and their just requirements...."

    c. *Modalities.* "In order to provide full autonomy to the inhabitants... the Israeli military government and its civilian administration will be withdrawn as soon as a self-governing authority has been freely elected by the inhabitants of these areas to replace the existing military government...."

    "To negotiate the details of a transitional arrangement the Government of Jordan will be invited to join the negotiations on the basis of this framework...."

    "The delegations of Egypt and Jordan may include Palestinians from the West Bank and Gaza or other Palestinians as mutually agreed...."

    "A withdrawal of Israeli armed forces will take place and there will be a redeployment of the remaining Israeli forces into specified security locations...."

    d . *The Next Stage.* "When the self-governing authority (administrative council) in the West Bank and Gaza is established and inaugurated, the transitional period of five years will begin...."

"As soon as possible, but not later than the third year after the beginning of the transitional period, negotiations will take place to determine the final status of the West Bank and Gaza and its relationship with its neighbours, and to conclude a peace treaty between Israel and Jordan by the end of the transitional period...."

"These negotiations will be conducted among Egypt, Israel, Jordan, and the elected representatives of the inhabitants of the West Bank and Gaza...."

This is the offer that Israel has made to the Palestinians. And this is the offer which Europe has spurned alongside those for whom the prospect of anything remotely resembling Arab-Israeli peace is sheer anathema. Instead Europe opted for a course "calling for the PLO... to be associated with the negotiations".

There is no better indication of the course which Europe has embarked upon and no worse indictment of the Venice Declaration than its omission of any mention of the Palestinian Covenant. As Camp David constitutes Israel's offer to the Palestinians so is the Covenant the PLO's "offer" to Israel. Here are *its* highlights:

1. *Objective.* "The liberation of Palestine is a national duty and it attempts to repel the Zionist and imperialist aggression against the Arab homeland, and aims at the elimination of Zionism in Palestine...."

2. *Principles.* "The partition of Palestine in 1947 and the establishment of the State of Israel are entirely illegal, regardless of the passage of time...."

"The Balfour Declaration, the Mandate for Palestine and everything that has been based upon them, are deemed null and void. Claims of historical or religious ties of Jews with Palestine are incompatible with the facts of history

208

and the true conception of what constitutes statehood. Judaism, being a religion, is not an independent nationality. Nor do Jews constitute a single nation with an identity of its own; they are citizens of the states to which they belong...."

3. *Modalities.* "Armed struggle is the only way to liberate Palestine. Thus it is the overall strategy, not merely a tactical phase. The Palestinian Arab people assert their absolute determination and firm resolution to continue their armed struggle and to work for an armed popular revolution for the liberation of their country and their return to it...."

"Commando action constitutes the nucleus of the Palestinian popular liberation war. This requires its escalation, comprehensiveness and mobilisation of all the Palestinian popular and educational efforts and their organization and involvement in the armed Palestinian revolution...."

4. *The Next Stage.* "The Jews who had normally resided in Palestine until the beginning of the Zionist invasion will be considered Palestinians."

"The liberation of Palestine will destroy the Zionist and imperialist presence and will contribute to the establishment of peace in the Middle East...."

Thus far the PLO's "offer" to Israel.

Suspicious and distrustful as we may be today of Europe's motives and actions we do not for a minute of course conceive it possible that Europe could now or ever be capable of actually endorsing this "offer" of the PLO to Israel. Likewise we accept Europe's protestations that its present efforts are aimed at securing a reform of the PLO's "offer". But in matters as potentially apocalyptic as these, intentions, good as they may be, are not only insufficient but can well pave the way to hell — in the literal sense of the word. In matters as exacting as these it is the practice which counts, and the practice is that Europe is on record today as willing to consider the PLO fit for association in a peace process and has declared this to be an integral part of its concept for the resolution of the Arab-Israel conflict without having secured even the slightest amendment to the PLO's offer: Rather it is the PLO which has succeeded in extracting from Europe this most far-reaching concession while maintaining the fullest fidelity to its Covenant. This is best reflected by Europe's appalling failure to make even the slightest reference to the Palestinian Covenant — not even as an "obstacle to peace", a designation apparently reserved for those notorious Israeli settlements where "no less" than 20,000 Israelis have settled in barely fourteen years (amidst a Palestinian Arab population of over a million!).

Does Europe seriously believe that having yielded so much in return for literally nothing has enhanced its chances of bringing about a reform of the PLO's "offer"? Or is not the PLO justified in holding fast to its original "offer" now that it has succeeded in extracting from Europe a document which accepts practically every Arab demand bar that which calls for the dismantling of Israel? Can the PLO be faulted for believing that with a little more push and shove, blackmail and intimidation, arson and terror, Europe will be brought to the point where — while steadfast in its support for "Israel's right to exist" — it will be willing to concede *the PLO* the right to deny Israel the right to exist and thus accept the PLO as a party to the negotiations with its Covenant intact? This is precisely the objective which the PLO has set for itself and from which it will not — and can not — flinch or deviate. Farouk Qaddumi, Head of the Political Department of the PLO, could not have made it more clear:

> We can never allow any party to interfere in our affairs, especially in two major matters: our non-recognition of Israel and our refusal to amend our national charter in any way. I hope I am making myself clear to everyone everywhere, especially to the European countries. We have said over and over again that we refuse to recognise Israel. This is unchangeable, permanent policy.
> (Interview with the Beirut weekly *Monday Morning*, April 9, 1981).

The choice before Europe is fast becoming clear and simple: will it choose to endorse and support Israel's offer to the Palestinians — the Camp David agreements — or will it allow itself to be dragged into acquiescing in the PLO's right to its Covenant? There is no middle ground between these two offers *and the chasm which separates them cannot and will not be bridged by any verbal acrobatics.* One offers a measured process of reconciliation and coexistence. The other offers total rejection and implacable enmity. One offers the gradual dissolution of an old and bitter conflict. The other seeks finite solutions and final confrontation.

Israel for its part can do no more and it will be futile to continue to harass and hound it to offer more than it has. Given Israel's unique strategic situation and the critical importance to Israel's security of the areas involved; given the continued enmity of all of Israel's eastern neighbours; given the vast arsenal of weapons in the hands of Arab countries and regimes which are sworn to wage endless war upon Israel no matter what it does or what it offers;

211

given the passionate attachment of all Israelis to the territories in question and the continued Israeli debate over
their future, Israel's offer is not just the only one it could
possibly make but also a magnanimous one.

Historians will one day pronounce on the manner in
which Europe failed to rally round the Camp David process as soon as it was launched, with half the verve and
enthusiasm which has since been generated around the
so-called "European Initiative". In the meantime contemporary observers might wish to ponder the possibility that
had all those who truly seek a just and viable end to the
Israeli-Palestinian conflict put all of their efforts behind
the Camp David process, we would now be approaching
the end of the first stage of the "Autonomy" and be
preparing to enter into "negotiations... to determine the
final status of the West Bank and Gaza and its relationship
with its neighbours"!

In spurning Israel's offer Europe has done enormous
damage to its credibility in the eyes of Israel, perhaps
beyond what is realised. Europe today is conceived by
Israel as pursuing a biased policy that is as impervious
to Israel's needs as it is to Israel's sensitivities. It is
seen as pursuing its own fleeting economic interests at the
expense of Israel's existential ones. It is looked upon as
willing and anxious to provide Israel's enemies with every
conceivable and inconceivable implement of war while
effectively denying Israel access to its armouries.

As the world begins to weigh the consequences of recycling atomic reactors and weapon-grade fissionable material for oil, it might do well also to take a fresh look at the
possible — if not certain — consequences of bartering
enormous amounts (now valued at 40 billion dollars a

212

year) of conventional arms for oil. The following comment in the 1981 Report by the Stockholm International Peace Research Institute might well serve as a good reference point.

Arms-for-oil as well as arms-for-uranium were by 1980 familiar terms of the arms trade. One of the latest examples was Iraq, which decided to give priority to its five largest arms suppliers outside the Socialist bloc, when the limited resumption of oil shipments was started in late 1980. These five countries were France, Brazil, Italy, Spain and Yugoslavia. For France, the export of arms represented one quarter of the oil bill in 1978. Similarly, it was reported that arms industry representatives from West Germany started negotiations in 1980 with Saudi Arabia, aimed at the supply of Leopard-2 tanks and the Tornado fighter in return for a Saudi guarantee of the supply of 40 per cent of West Germany's oil requirements during the 1980s.

If many Israelis today are driven to believe that friendlessness is an essential element of the Jewish condition and that they can trust none but themselves, then the responsibility for this unhappy state of affairs lies neither with Israel nor with its enemies but rather with many of Israel's European friends for having failed to lend their support and encouragement to a people's genuine and well-intentioned attempt to seek a way out of its enormous problems and predicaments, precisely when this support and encouragement was most needed and just as equally deserved. If such is our mood at home and our view of the world outside, responsibility for this should be apportioned to no small degree between the respective govern-

213

ments of the European Economic Community. For, paradoxical as it may sound, Israel is hardly oblivious of Europe. Rejecting as it does Europe's presumptions to determine for it the conditions and parameters for its future, Israel is a nation traumatized by its European past and therefore deeply sensitive to Europe.

No small share of responsibility for Israel's mistrustful attitude towards Europe today belongs to much — though by no means all — of Europe's media for having been engaged for some time now in what has come close to verging on a frenzied hounding of every aspect of Israeli life and conduct leaving no blemish unbloated, no fault uninflated, no problem unmagnified while increasingly omitting all reference to what is good and decent about it. In so doing the media has played — unwittingly though it may have been — into the hands of those who seek to propagate such an image of Israel as justification for their mandate for its destruction.

Be that as it may, let there be no misunderstanding about one point: there are certain things Israel can live with and others it cannot live without and Israel alone is the judge of what these are. To attempt to push us beyond what we consider critical to our interests is to meet with our fullest resistance. Small and beleaguered though it may be, Israel possesses substantial power and resilience as well as unbounded determination to survive. We have come a long way and mean to go an even longer one and we also have the wherewithal to ensure that we do so.

Thank you.

Address at the Yad Vashem Ceremony

The Koninklijk Instituut voor de Tropen
Amsterdam, November 23, 1977

We are gathered here today in order to express our deep respect and admiration for twenty-eight gallant Dutch men and women, who in the dark years of the Second World War dared to challenge the bestiality that raged around them and at grave risk to themselves and their families gave shelter to persecuted Jewish men, women and children, especially children.

Altogether these valiant men and women represent some 25,000 Dutch families which gave their homes and their hearts to approximately 25,000 Dutch Jews in those terrible times in the early forties. In addition, an estimated 1,000 members of the Dutch resistance dedicated themselves fully to the task of saving Jews and finding hiding places for them. Of these 25,000 Jews approximately two-thirds actually survived the war.

Small as these figures are when pitted against the enormity of the catastrophe which befell the Jews of The Netherlands, they nonetheless evoke a saga of heroism that has earned for the Dutch people the everlasting gratitude and affection of the Jewish people.

Barely thirty-five years have passed since those curfew hours in 1942–43, when solitary trams could be heard making their pitiful way through the streets of this city carrying away their load of silent men, women and child-

215

ren who until moments before had been such an integral and vibrant part of it. What went through their minds? What foreboding did they have? What fears gripped them? What anguish did they feel when they saw their own neighbourhoods flashing by, where, until only hours before, they had lived just as generations of their families had lived? What did they feel when they saw the shops and workshops where they had toiled and earned their living, and schools where classes would somehow resume the following morning, though some seats would be suddenly vacant. Terrified as they must have been, they did not and could not suspect the fate that awaited them. Most of them were never to come back.

In the forthcoming eighth volume of his monumental work *The Kingdom of The Netherlands During the Second World War,* Lou de Jong reveals that out of 107,000 Dutch Jews deported eastwards barely 5,000 survived. The specific details are even more harrowing: of 42,945 sent to Auschwitz between July 15, 1942 and February 23, 1943, 85 survived. Out of 34,313 Dutch Jews sent to Sobibor between March and July 1943, 19 came back. The rest perished, some in the heroic uprising which took place in this perhaps most notorious of the Nazi death camps. And so it was in the other camps to which Jews from The Netherlands were sent along with a major part of European Jewry in order to make Europe *Judenrein.* And thus was inflicted upon the Jewish people the most devastating massacre in its history.

Thirty-five years have gone by and much of this is now forgotten by a great many people, by some as a normal consequence of human nature, by others deliberately. We in Israel shall never forget. And this for two reasons: first, because we owe it to our dead; second because we owe it to ourselves. Genocide has been perpetrated in our times systematically and methodically, in full view and with very little if anything being done either to prevent or to stop it. This is the lesson that we have vowed to pass from generation to generation. And for good reason — for there are still those who preach genocide against the Jews of Israel, effigies of Jews are still being burnt in all too familiar circumstances, passengers on one hijacked plane are subjected to a "selection" process not unlike that practiced in Birkenau while those of another hijacked plane are terrorized for the crime of bearing Jewish-sounding names. And the United Nations General Assembly is still the scene of a deliberate and systematic smear campaign against Israel where nations vote en masse in favour of most anti-Israel resolutions in circumstances that might well be described as a political pogrom. In this connection, well-meaning friends might want to consider the possibility that in lending their support to some of these resolutions they are hardly advancing the cause of peace nor helping the task of peacemaking, not to speak of the grievous injury they cause Israel itself.

As we repeat this vow today we do so, however, with renewed hope and prayer in our hearts. A hope and a prayer that I know all of you here and millions of people — many millions of people — in Israel, in Egypt, elsewhere in the Middle East and throughout the world share. It is the profound hope and the fervent prayer that the momentous events which we have just witnessed in Israel this week* will mark the dawn of a new era in the relations between

* Signing of the Israel-Egypt peace treaty.

Arab and Israeli, an era which will see an end to the strife and the violence and which will before long be marked by the highest standards and ideals of peace as established by the prophets of Israel many centuries ago.

And it may well be that when history records these historic days it will reveal that the resolve to put an end to the wars was sealed as the leaders of Egypt and Israel stood together in Yad Vashem in Jerusalem in silent memory of the millions of our brothers and sisters, the victims of man's inhumanity to man. That, I know, will also be the finest reward the people we honour here today could ever wish for.

The Case for
British-Israeli Friendship

Address to the York Anglo-Israel Friendship Society
February 23, 1982

Mr. Chairman, Your Grace, distinguished members of the clergy, councillors, ladies and gentlemen. We are meeting tonight under the auspices of the York Anglo-Israel Friendship Society and in the name of British-Israel friendship. I can think of no better auspices. We are also meeting in order to express support for two most worthy projects that have been sponsored by the York Anglo-Israel Friendship Society.

The "York Project" is dedicated to the promotion of Arab-Israeli understanding in the most meaningful way by bringing together Jewish and Arab high-school students in Jerusalem. There can be no better investment in the future than in the promotion of amity between those to whom it belongs.

The second project which we have come to laud here tonight is "The Annual Essay Competition for Sixth Formers" in York which has already made it possible for ten youngsters from this great historic city to visit Israel for six weeks, when they will get to know the land and the people and their own peers there. Again, I can think of no better way of ensuring the continued flourishing of British-Israel friendship than to enable youngsters from both

219

countries to be introduced to each other and to their respective societies as well as to the rich heritage of friendship between our two peoples.

Ours in an historic relationship based on a wide commonality of ethics, norms and shared experiences extending across generations. Speaking at a debate in the House of Lords on July 22, 1922, Lord Balfour said:

> Surely it is in order that we may send a message to every land where the Jewish race has been scattered, a message which will tell them that Christendom is not oblivious of their faith, is not unmindful of the service they have rendered to the great religions of the world... and that we desire, to the best of our ability, to give them the opportunity of developing in peace and quietness, under British rule, those great gifts which hitherto they have been compelled... only to bring to fruition in countries which know not their language and belong not to their race.... That is the aim which lay at the root of the policy I am trying to defend; and though it is defensible on every ground, that is the ground that chiefly moves me.

Three themes can be detected in Lord Balfour's words: First, the deep religious identification with the age-old Jewish struggle for redemption. This was, and no doubt continues to be, central to the tradition of British-Israel friendship. This is how Chaim Weizmann once perceived it:

> The fundamental underlying idea which led up to the Balfour Declaration was a desire to right a Jewish wrong, and it is not an accident that it was Great Britain which understood most deeply this idea, because one

does not read the Bible for centuries without becoming saturated with its ideas. And saturated as the British people were with the images, pictures and prophecies of the Old Testament, they understood what has been treasured up in the Jewish people, and they understood it as a natural phenomenon, an actual physical return of the Jews to Palestine.

Lord Balfour's second theme was clearly the underlying moral drive to help put right the wrong that was done to the Jewish people in centuries of bitter exile. Recalling a conversation he had with Balfour in 1917 the late Harold Nicolson quotes him as having said on that occasion:

The Jews are the most gifted race that mankind has seen since the Greeks of the fifth century. They have been exiled, scattered and oppressed.... If we can find them an asylum, a safe home, in their native land, then the full flowering of their genius will burst forth and propagate.... The submerged Jews of the ghettoes of Eastern Europe will in Palestine find a new life and develop a new and powerful identity. And the educated Jews from all over the world will render the University of Jerusalem a centre of intellectual life and a radiant nurse of science and the arts".

The third discernible theme is Balfour's astute recognition of the British interest in identifying with the Jewish struggle for national liberation. Another British statesman, David Lloyd George, put it this way:

There we were, confronted with your people in every country of the world, very powerful. You may say you have been oppressed and persecuted — that has been

221

your power! You have been hammered into fine steel....
And therefore we wanted your help. We thought it
would be very useful.

A natural Christian affinity with the people of the Bible,
the urge to help put right an historic wrong, and the British
interest in identifying with both, combined to form the
rationale for the Balfour Declaration in its day. These
three themes are as valid today as they were then and
together continue to make a convincing case for British-
Israel friendship today.

Now, as then, ours is a relationship which continues to
rest on a foundation of common norms and ethics. In an
increasingly cynical, intolerant and authoritarian world,
our two countries continue to be committed to a philosophy in which man, born in the image of God, is not a
mere instrumentality in the hands of government but
rather the be-all and the end-all of social and political
organization — the ultimate beneficiary of national exer-
tion and therefore its natural arbiter. We believe not in the
oppression of man for the sake of some illusory common
good but rather in the betterment and flowering of man as
the only object of common effort. We, like you, therefore
continue to persist in our unflagging commitment to
democracy as the only system known to man which is
predicated on respect for man. As such our two countries
are members of a proportionately diminishing small band
of nations in this world of ours. Out of one hundred and
fifty-seven member-states of the United Nations only
thirty-six can legitimately claim title to a democratic form
of government. In the Middle East Israel is the only country which has inscribed fidelity to democracy as a central

national tenet. This is hardly in dissonance with our ancient precepts and traditions. While others may have articulated democracy in political terms better than we did in our time, nowhere was it more emphatically laid down and more lastingly forged than by the lawgivers and prophets of the Bible. Just as equally nowhere was democracy translated into a living reality as in this great country of yours.

Espousing the cause of a dispersed and persecuted people kept alive by the promise of ultimate redemption is no less valid a cause today than it was in Balfour's days. His generation was moved by the plight of Eastern European Jews fleeing from the brutal oppression of Tzarist Russia. That was the order of the enormity which Balfour in his day felt his moral obligation to put right. The world however did not stand still. The war that was to end all wars and the peace that was to bring justice to all nations were apparently not meant to take account of the Jews' plight and plea. They were yet to be struck by the greatest catastrophe ever to befall any nation in modern times and perhaps in all times. And herein too lies a deep British-Israeli bond.

Historical research into the destruction of the Jews of Europe has revealed and confirmed most if not all of our fears and suspicions concerning their abandonment by the rest of the world and thus also convinced us yet again of some profound Jewish axioms about the unique experience of being Jewish in a less than hospitable world. At the same time Jews and Israelis will never forget the role played by this country in standing up to and ultimately triumphing over the beast that threatened to devour us all — and which alas succeeded in reducing to ashes no less

223

than one-third of our people. That beacon of light which continued to shine bright in these isles when the rest of the world was plunged into the blackest of darkness was also the one remaining hope for the Jewish people. As the sensation of Jewish loneliness reached its quintessence we knew at least that there was one decent people which also stood "alone" against the forces of evil.

Today Israel provides for its own defence. We are masters of our own destiny. We are the protectors of our own people through the instrumentality which has been forged by us in the thirty-four years since the fulfilment of the Jewish dream. Ours is a viable and powerful state capable of ensuring that man's inhumanity to his Jewish brother will neither be permitted nor left unpunished. We are home and safe at last in our ancient homeland. Moreover — to use Lloyd George's words — we have indeed been "hammered into fine steel" and are, as he clearly expected and anticipated, able to offer help.

Impressions, notions and deliberate distortions to the contrary, a powerful Israel in the Middle East is hardly a Western liability. Consider the theoretical — indeed highly theoretical — scenario of a Middle East without a strong and viable Israel exuding an aura of strength. How many of the West's friends — albeit not yet our friends — would survive such a Middle East? Compare the turmoil and bloodshed which presently attend the crucial struggle for the Persian — or Arabian if you will — Gulf, the results of which may well determine the struggle for Europe itself, with the relative stability at the other end of the Middle East where Israel is. Here alone in the Middle East is where the central theme and enterprise is the business of peacemaking and here alone in the Middle East is where vital

Western interests are nowhere nearly as gravely challenged as they are elsewhere in the area. For here and here alone is where there is an Israel exuding credible power and deterrence into its immediate surroundings. Here and here alone in the Middle East is where the West can indeed take for granted the fidelity of a country among whose foremost national interests is the security and prosperity of the free world.

Friendless though we have been all of these centuries we seek to force friendship on no one. Friendship must spring from recognised empathies, affinities and close interests. And yet few countries can claim such a measure of common ground as that which is represented by our respective histories and heritage as well as the essential compatibility of our struggle for a secure future for our peoples.

All this was foreseen and described many years before Balfour by one of Britain's greatest statesmen — himself a scion of the Jewish people. In the final chapter of his recent and revealing book *Disraeli's Grand Tour,* Lord Blake quotes from a remarkable conversation, sometime in January 1851, between Disraeli and Lord Stanley, who was to become the 15th Earl of Derby.

The subject was the restoration of the Jews to their own land. Disraeli said that the country had excellent natural resources.

"All it wanted was labour and protection for the labourer: the ownership of the soil might be bought from Turkey: money would be forthcoming: the Rothschilds and leading Hebrew capitalists would all help: the Turkish empire was falling into ruin: ... all that was necessary was to establish colonies with rights over the soil and security from ill treatment. The question of nationality might wait until these had taken hold."

This conversation took place in what was then Lord Carrington's park near Wycombe in the County of Buckinghamshire.

Concluding his book Lord Blake writes:

One cannot doubt where Disraeli would have stood. He surely would have welcomed the [Balfour] Declaration and would have been overjoyed at Allenby's entrance into Jerusalem. He would have remembered his own words about the night breeze on the Mount of Olives — "the haunting voice of the prophets mourning over a city that they could not save" — and he would have been thrilled at the thought that it might be saved after all.

On Wallenberg and Jewish Survival

*Remarks at the Zionist Central Council and
the Jewish Representative Council of Greater Manchester*

March 1, 1981

Many of us have already met earlier this afternoon when
we participated in a very moving and meaningful meeting
convened by this community in order to pay homage to a
remarkable man — Raoul Wallenberg. A gallant Swede
who in the darkest hours of our people — literally the
twilight of a third of our people — alone walked the streets
of Budapest, then under the satanic rule of the Germans
and their Hungarian cohorts, and singlehandedly saved
thousands of Jews from certain annihilation. It is estimated that Raoul Wallenberg was instrumental in saving
no less than one hundred thousand Jews, a feat without
precedent or parallel, for which he deserves the everlasting
gratitude and admiration of the Jewish people — indeed of
the entire world. As we pay homage to this man today, we
do so in the fervent hope and prayer that he is still alive and
that he will emerge one day from that cell or camp in the
Soviet Union where he is incarcerated, so that we can
shower upon him our gratitude and our love and admiration. Raoul Wallenberg will however understand why we
cannot be content only with thanksgiving for his heroic
feat and why, as Jews, it is incumbent on us also to draw
certain lessons from his story. For there is a frightening

227

and horrifying aspect to Wallenberg's lonely epic, and that aspect is its very loneliness!

Wallenberg represented nobody but himself. Nobody but his conscience. Nobody but his own personal humanity. He was not despatched by anyone to carry out what became his mission. He set off on his journey without end at his own initative, of his own free will and in response to a dictate of his personal morality. He paraded as if he were a representative of a great power. He bargained with the Germans as if he had the backing of massive forces and as though he controlled powers of terrible retribution and retaliation. The amazing but not necessarily incomprehensible thing is that the Germans took his warning and his threats seriously. They *dared* not call his bluff and allowed him to take Jews off trains and out of camps — literally to pry them out of the sealed wagons that were about to set off for that satanic place. And here is the lesson: If Raoul Wallenberg could singlehandedly save a hundred thousand Hungarian Jews then all that was needed in order to save all of the Jews of Europe was sixty Wallenbergs! No more! All it would have taken was sixty people like Wallenberg ready and willing to face up to that devilish regime and to demand from it the lives of the Jews of Europe. Wallenberg did it but he was the only one. Not only was he practically the only *individual* who had the courage and the decency to do what he did but there was not another *government* that was willing to do what he did. If one solitary man could do what Wallenberg did, could not great powers have done at least as much? One *single* man saved a hundred thousand Jews. How easy it could have been for mighty powers to have saved the rest! If only they had dared, if only they had cared. But they did not.

Not one of them. At no time during the Second World War was the saving of Jews a war objective of any of the Allied Powers. Jews were to be saved as a by-product of the Allied victory, as the logical consequence of the freeing of the continent of Europe from the yoke of the Nazi oppressor. But when the yoke of the Nazi oppressor was removed, there were no more Jews. Today the Continent of Europe is the largest graveyard in Jewish history. A vast Jewish graveyard, extending from the sea to the Urals.

This is why it is incomprehensible to us that Israel should today have to protect itself against European efforts which may compromise her very ability to survive. It is literally beyond our understanding how Europeans could take such cavalier risks with the most vital interests of the State of Israel knowing as they must how fickle *they* can be and how imperilled *we* can be. If certain European initiatives were to be realised today, the effect would be to deprive Israel of its ability and capacity to defend itself and to make it dependent for its very survival on the graces and good will of a Europe that stood by while its Jews were obliterated before its eyes. We do not have the exact details of the so-called "European Initiative" because we are not privy to them. Though they affect our very lives, security and future, they are being deliberated in our absence. This has happened before in Europe. We recall another little country whose future was discussed. Its representatives were kept waiting outside as its security and viability was undermined with cynicism and disdain by the same European countries which now presume to tell us where our borders should run, who should be our neighbours and what should happen to our capital. In Venice they pronounced the murderous PLO fit for "association" in a

229

peace process. In Luxembourg they concluded that Israel should withdraw to the pre-1967 lines, including East Jerusalem. In the territories to be evacuated the PLO is to lead the Palestinians to so-called self-determination. That is the European prescription.

If Europe is to be allowed to have its way today as it was allowed to do in 1938 the result will be identical. Like Czechoslovakia, Israel will no longer be able to provide for its security. However, unlike Czechoslovakia, Israel will not survive such an emasculation. The Czechs could survive in 1938, 1948 and 1968. We cannot.

It is said that we are a traumatised people but we have every reason and justification to be so. Our traumas are not a figment of our imagination. They are a product of our reality. Today as in the past, in the future as in the present, Israel's existence cannot be protected and safeguarded except by Israel alone. To confirm us in this conviction we need not draw only on our pre-state days and the harrowing years of the Second World War experience. We have stood alone since 1948 as we have done before. We were tested alone and we prevailed alone. Ours has been a lonely journey from the very beginning. It will always remain so. And that is why we must always be capable of ensuring our own defence literally with our bare hands and the weapons they can wield. We trust no one. The virtuous and lonely Raoul Wallenberg would understand why.

Whatever Europe has in store for us will not come into being, because we are determined to resist it. We will prevail because, unlike Europe, we are *not* engaged in the protection of a fleeting economic interest. The interests we protect are existential ones. Survival — that is what is at stake. And so when their fleeting economic interests are matched and pitted against our existential interests, I can assure you that it will be our existential ones that will prevail for such is the intensity and the magnitude and the force that can be wielded for the protection of existential interests.

The "European initiative" is bound to be no more than a mere episode — a pinprick. We shall be tested and we shall be tried but we shall prevail. Hopefully, wiser counsels may yet prevail and matters will not be allowed to come to a head. There is no real justification for the pitting of European and Israeli interests. We believe that our interests and those of Europe are not incompatible but rather very compatible. Not only because we are a decent country and a democratic country in the best traditions of Western European democracy, but because in the final analysis Israel is an important repository of pro-Western power in our volatile part of the world and the only steady, cohesive, stable country on which the West can rely with confidence. It is hoped, also, that a reasonable measure of understanding for Israel's interests will be revealed by those who presently do not demonstrate such understanding and seek to impose upon Israel a solution which they perceive as consonant with their interest but which clashes brutally with ours.

But we Jews must look beyond all this. We must look beyond this latest European antic and the manner in which it will be resisted and rebuffed and rendered a passing episode. As we brace ourselves for the possible test and challenge that may lie ahead we must ask ourselves some hard, uncompromising questions. These can be reduced to two principal ones: How secure is Israel? What more can

we do to secure it? The answer to the first question is that
Israel is secure. Israel is a strong country possessing
immense power. It is a country that has held its own in the
face of incredible odds and not only has it been able to hold
its own but it has managed at the same time also to create
and build and develop a remarkable society, a highly
sophisticated economy and a safe home for its people. The
answer to the second question is that secure as it is Israel
needs to be secured further. When I say "secured" I do not
mean merely in material terms. I am not referring once
again to financial support. Nor do I have in mind any kind
of abstract moral support, important as all of these are.
Money is needed, support is essential, encouragement and
solidarity are critical. But it is time we understood something: Israel needs reinforcement. *It needs more Jews!*
There are not enough of us there. Those of us who man the
battlements of Israel, the bastion of the People of Israel,
are few and they need their ranks increased! This is how
Yizhar Smilansky, one of our great writers, has recently
put it: "There is one thing which precedes all else," he said
in the daily *Davar* of February 6, "it precedes foreign
affairs, defence, economics, peace agreements, everything
— it is the Jewish people". So says a vintage Israeli from
Rehovoth. The Jewish people, that is the most important
thing. And he goes on to say: "What is it that could serve as
the theme of the new era on whose threshold we may be? It
is none other than four million Jews in Eretz Israel within
the next five years. Simple as it is unbelievable. Believable
but not easy. It seems too little and yet it appears a pipe
dream at the same time. It is an aim which is dream and
reality combined. If in four, five years, four million Jews
live here securely, the history of the Jewish people will be

different and so will the region we live in. The regional balance will change and the balance of peace will be secured. Can you ask for more? Only this: if we know, believe and act we will also come to be proud for we shall have willed it to be".

It is within the capacity of the Jewish people today to answer Israel's central and most critical need. We *know* the answer: *all of us* know the answer; every Jew wherever he is knows the answer to all of Israel's problems. We all know exactly, precisely almost mathematically, how we can secure the country and the State of Israel: If the Jewish people outside Israel, which today numbers twelve million, were to give us in ten years one million Jews, Israel will be secured forever. Forever! No one shall dare raise a hand against us. No one shall point a finger at us. We shall be credible, powerful, strong, everlasting. It is within the grasp of the Jewish people to provide the answer, to fulfill Israel's most vital requirement. And that requirement is: More Jews in Israel!

I have quoted from Yizhar Smilansky. I shall now quote from another of our great writers — Amos Oz. Amos Oz is also one of those sons of Eretz Israel. A son of the sun that shines upon our Land of Israel. And he is deeply troubled. He is troubled about the same things. Notice how *we Israelis* are consumed with constant concern about one subject: the Jewish people. It is the number-one item on our list of priorities. Not only because we need Jews in order to reinforce us but because we are convinced and confirmed in our belief that this is the only way to ensure Jewish peoplehood. That really is our job. This is what you have told us we should do. This is what we have been charged with by the Jewish people and Jewish history: the ensuring of Jewish peoplehood until the end of time and beyond. And this is what Amos Oz says: "The gravest danger to the future of Zionism and to our very existence is not from the Arabs and the outside world. It stems from two sources, from the ideology of 'galut' which has raised its head in recent years, and from the loss of faith here and in the people of Israel at home. The 'galut' has raised its head not only in terms of financial remittances which it makes available to us but also in the attacks on the Zionist enterprise. We must fight this battle with full force because it is the battle for our sons, for those who have left us and for those who will never leave."

There is a new fad today: to relegate Israel to a position of parity with the Diaspora. To relegate Israel to that position not so much as part of an ideological concept; Those who so label us are incapable of great ideological conceptualisation. Theirs is a pragmatic argument: We Israelis are not as good as we claim to be. We are beset with problems, blemished by imperfections. How dare we claim precedence, primacy? How dare we have claims on the Western Diaspora?

Now we are not without blemish. But then who are we? Let me tell you who we are. We are the social-welfare station of the Jewish people. That is who we are. We received the sick and the maimed, the poor, the diseased, the blind and the invalids of all of our people. And we are expected to integrate them, to resuscitate them and to convert them into constructive citizens. All this on top of fighting five wars in thirty-two years, creating an agriculture out of a wilderness, inventing an industry out of nothing, building, constructing, developing, teaching, healing, comforting and above all creating a nation out of

234

refugees and escapees. And lo and behold! Standards have
fallen and blemishes have been noted. So much so in fact as
to make us undeserving of Western immigration. We do
not, it seems, measure up to Western Diaspora standards!

There is a grain of truth in all this. The society of Israel
has changed. It is not what it used to be. We are no longer a
band of heroic pioneers but have become a blend and a
composite of all of the strands and strains of the Jewish
people. We have been saddled with two thousand years of
the consequences of the persecution of Jews and now there
are those who complain that we are imperfect. If you want
to secure Israel — and you *must* secure Israel because
Israel will always remain the subject of testing, of challenge, and Israel will always live in danger — then you
must help us erase the blemishes and remove the imperfections by helping us raise the standards of Israeli society to
the level we all expect it to maintain.

But to do this we must have some of the best equipped
and qualified of the Jewish people. And so we say to you of
the so-called Western Diaspora: you cannot have your
cake and eat it too. You cannot expect us to be able to
deliver the goods punctually and perfectly unless you join
the fray and help do it. We have done so until now but it
has been an enormous effort and the burden has not been
shared equitably. We have been saddled with all of the
problems. We are not complaining. That is what we are
here for. That is what the state is all about — a haven for
persecuted Jews. But there is a limit to what we can do all
by ourselves. We need reinforcement. What awaits us —
the "European initative" today and those that will follow
— calls for the very best in us. We will confront all these
confidently and deal with them efficiently. We shall over-

235

come. But we need help and help today means reinforcements. As we look to the future let us therefore act together
in order to ease Israel's burden. The securing of Israel is
the business not only of Israel but of the entire Jewish
people. "If we know, believe and act" — if the entire
Jewish people believe and act — "we will also come to be
proud for we shall have willed it to be".

The Threat to
International Economic Stability

Address at a
luncheon given by the Labour Friends of Israel to
Delegates of the TUC Annual Congress
Blackpool, September 8, 1981

In the story of British-Israel relations one dimension
stands out in particular — the abiding friendship and
solidarity which exist between our working people and the
warm fraternal relations which bind our respective great
trade-union movements. This is a most natural relationship for it rests both on the commonality of our working
men's interests and our joint fidelity to the norms and
ethics of free democratic societies. We in Israel will always
be indebted to you for blazing the trail to parliamentary
democracy to which we have remained true and faithful.

It is only right that we should take for granted our own
and each other's adherence to the democratic system for
neither of us could possibly conceive of any alternative or
substitute. And yet in Israel's case it is perhaps not entirely
out of place to stress this essential feature of our form of
government. Unlike you in Britain, we in Israel are the
only society in our part of the world that is so constituted.
In the entire continent of Asia there are only two more
countries which can legitimately take pride in belonging to
that small band of free democratic societies. And when it

237

comes to that crucial attribute of any society laying claim to membership in our ever shrinking fraternity, namely a vital, vibrant and free trade-union movement, there is not one country in either Asia or Africa that can boast of such a remarkable labour federation as the Histadrut.

Governments come and go. Political parties are voted into and out of office but the Histadrut remains a central pillar of Israel's national life. One of the most remarkable features of the rough-and-tumble of Israeli politics in recent years has been the growing competition of *all* major political parties for the support and endorsement of the working men and women of Israel. No government is conceivable in Israel unless it is able to articulate and advance the interests and goals of Israel's working people.

Israel's continued and abiding fidelity to the ideals of freedom and democracy are deserving of recognition in view of another unique feature of the Israeli condition: No other country in recent history has ever had to contend with such threats and dangers to itself and consequently also to its normative fabric. And yet rarely, if ever, has a country which has had to rely on military excellence for its very survival been as safe and as immune to encroachment upon its democratic institutions as Israel is.

Unfortunately this is not the image projected by the mass media of the free world — and hardly excluding the British. The overwhelmingly positive aspects of Israel, its innate morality and decency, are not only ignored but given short shrift. Israel is the only country in the world whose existence is being threatened in the most direct and physical sense. In thirty-two years of national existence we have had to fight no less than five major wars while in between our citizens — men, women and children — have

238

been subjected to daily assault and harassment by an entity publicly committed to the total denial to Israel and its people of the most basic of human rights — sheer physical existence. Of late we also seem to have come to enjoy the distinction — according to a curious British diplomatic exercise — of being the only country whose right to exist can become the subject of "conditional recognition!" And yet it is we who are the neighbourhood bullies, the danger to peace and, worst of all, a threat to international economic stability.

Let us consider that last charge which is increasingly being levelled at us, namely of posing a threat to everybody's economic prosperity. Is it really we who imperil your well-being? Is it little Israel which is sapping the resources of the free world and undermining its very stability?

According to a report just issued by the OECD, the number of unemployed in OECD countries is expected to reach in the second half of 1982 the staggering number of 26.25 million working men and women — 19% more than two years earlier. Europe is likely to be worse hit with an increase in unemployment of more than one-quarter to at least 9.25% of the labour force, which is no less than 15 million people out of a job compared with 11.6 million last year. Most disturbing is the figure for jobless youth which is expected to reach over 20% in France, Britain and Italy. All this adds up to one of the most alarming problems of our times and has justly become the subject of widespread controversy, over its root causes as well. Curiously there seems to be a pact of silence about one possible if not certain root cause, namely the impoverishment of rich and poor alike by the systematic syphoning off of riches and

239

resources by the economic blackmailers of our time — the oil producers.

Where has all the money gone — that which could have been channeled into job creation, capital investment, technological innovation, the maintenance and improvement of infrastructures, not to speak of the protection and expansion of the social services? Here are some clues:

Between 1974–1979 the trade surplus of OPEC countries reached the mind-boggling figure of $431 billion. In 1979 alone that surplus was of the order of $120 billion while the estimates for last year are for a similar figure (the recession has "hit" the oilmen too!).

While the industrialised world and the developing nations both face ever grimmer economic prospects of rising inflation and growing unemployment one country — Saudi Arabia — with a population of barely six million, is in a position to allocate over the next five years almost $500 billion for Saudi "development projects", i.e. almost $100 billion per million of population per year! (Talk of fair distribution of wealth!)

What are some of these development projects? In 1980 alone, Saudi Arabia budgeted $20.7 billion for military expenditure. Altogether over the five-year period in question Saudi Arabia is expected to invest no less than $140 billion in such "development projects" as planes, tanks, missiles, airfields, naval craft and facilities and everything else that the free world could possibly offer it in what has become the most remarkable case of military procurement in history! Another prominent oil producer seems to be capable of doing all this and more. In addition to amassing the third-largest arsenal of weapons in the Middle East, Libya also has enough left over for financing an interna-

240

tional terror network as well as the development of what has come to be known as the "Islamic Bomb" (atomic) now reportedly on the verge of realisation.

Crushing as the consequences of such a diversion and wastage of resources and manufacturing capacity are to the industrialised world, they are literally catastrophic for the genuinely developing countries:

In 1973 the developing countries spent $4 billion on oil imports. In 1980 the figure reached $47 billion — an increase of 1,075% compared with a total increase in exports for the same period of 188%. In 1973 the trade imbalance of the developing world was $17.5 billion. By 1979 it had reached $73.5 billion.

By comparison OPEC coffers held by 1980 no less than $385 billion of surplus money, much of which (70%) was held on short-term speculative deposits in Western banks. The entire OPEC allocation of aid to developing countries in 1980 was $4.7 billion of which 70% went to Arab countries and mostly for arms purchases.

Nothing can demonstrate better the plight of the developing world — and the rest of the world, for that matter — than the following figure: It took seven-tenths of a bushel of wheat to buy one barrel of oil in 1973. In 1980 it took more than seven bushels of wheat to buy that same barrel of oil. Is it any wonder that the industrialised world is spiralled into ever-growing inflation and unemployment while the developing world is reduced to starvation?

And yet the common wisdom prevailing and daily being aired by the media of the West is that it is none other than Israel's policies which threaten international economic stability. If only Israel would yield and accept the counselling of friends and the dictates of enemies and divest itself

241

of its capacity to continue to defend itself then the world would be safe. If only Israel would give up its remaining critical strategic assets and allow East Jerusalem to become the seat of government of a certain genocidal organization then maybe that Saudi Prince, who is reported to have recently collected no less than $4 billion (*billion*!) commission for his good offices in facilitating a major oil transaction, would promise to stop doing so.

What are those $4 billion and all the other hundreds of billions of dollars amassed by the Arab oil producers? They are none other than the equivalent of the oceans of sweat of millions of workers all over the world; the sum total of billions of workdays invested in the desperate struggle to recycle precious national wealth for oil; the other billions of workdays evaporate as the world fails to keep up this mad race and the remaining billions of workdays which go into the production of ever more efficient death implements and machines for which the Arab world is currently the third-largest customer after the two superpowers. The Arab countries today possess more tanks than NATO, almost as many planes as NATO and more soldiers than NATO — all threatening only one possible adversary — Israel. And we are the neighbourhood bullies, the intransigent enemies of peace.

The danger to international economic stability is not this or that Israeli policy — controversial as they might be — just as it is not we who threaten the wealth of nations. Rather it is *we* who are the victims of the application of the most massive accumulation of economic power that the world has ever known for the purpose of coercing peoples and governments into turning their backs on a beleaguered people of three and a half million men, women and children. At stake therefore is not only the economic prosperity of Europe, the free world and the developing countries but also their decency and morality, for if ever they were to succumb to this ruthless economic pressure and combine to try to deliver little Israel to its persecutors the world would be guilty of the second attempt in this century on the life — no more, no less — of the Jewish people. But surely this will never come to pass, both because we will not permit it and because no decent working man or woman could ever tolerate it.

Britain, America and Israel

Speech to the New York United Jewish Appeal
London, September 12, 1981

At the risk of being presumptuous may I too welcome you to Britain and especially to its Jewish community. You are the guests of quite a remarkable community: proud of our common heritage, faithful to its traditions and deeply committed to the cause of Israel. Truly a gallant and valiant Jewry, responding courageously to the challenge of these times of crisis for Israel and the Jewish people everywhere.

You should know that what might loosely be called the view from Europe is very different from what you are accustomed to back in the United States. The circumstances and atmosphere on the continent of Europe in which the struggle for the peace of Israel is waged are not easy. They are in fact quite harsh and often cynical and contemptuous. There are of course gradations and variations but common to all of Europe today is the notion that recycling the most critical Israeli interests for the good graces of one's Arab financial and economic brokers is a perfectly acceptable formula. There are those who have no compunctions about publicly declaring their subscription to this political philosophy. Others cover it up self-righteously with a self-assumed obligation to put right the great wrong that we Jews have allegedly done to our Arab neighbours.

244

All of this may not be entirely unfamiliar to you. Such ideas have been known to be voiced and actively advocated on your side of the Atlantic. And yet there is one critical difference between the American and the European positions. Europe — in the guise of the European Economic Community — has for many years now done absolutely nothing either to help Israel withstand the staggering Arab onslaught against it nor has Europe made even the slightest contribution to the effort of hurling back tides of enmity and to the making of the first Arab-Israeli peace. While the United States has been willing to incur the wrath of this or that tin-pot Arab dictator — and a combination of these — and helped to enable Israel to defend itself by itself, Europe has been maintaining an arms embargo on Israel ever since the Yom Kippur War. Similarly as the United States put all of its prestige and backing behind the Camp David agreements — which would never had been realised without the United States in the first place — most of Europe was content to snigger and snort if not to complain outright that Camp David had not solved all of the problems of the Middle East in one fell swoop and provided "only" for peace between Egypt and Israel — a triviality in the eyes of some Europeans and a hindrance in the view of others.

This is not only disappointing but also tragic for if anybody owes us anything it is the continent of Europe which barely one generation ago destroyed practically all of its Jews and should at the very least therefore know better than to engage in the pursuit of policies which if ever realised could undermine Israel's very ability to survive. In the case of Britain this is especially painful for this is not only that decent land which one generation ago stood

245

alone as the only beacon of light in a world that had been plunged into abysmal darkness, but also the country in which were registered some of the most important chapters of this century in the Jewish people's millennia-old struggle for national liberation. Unfortunately, one is compelled to report that not only is this country actively engaged in advancing policies and concepts that are deeply injurious to Israel's most vital interests but of late one finds oneself incredulously detecting tones and notes that are a throwback to that most bitter chapter in British-Israel relations when Britain no less than actively sought to thwart the establishment of a Jewish state. Reading some of the British press these days one wonders whether we are not in 1947–1948 instead of 1981. Even the "Palestine Question" — as distinct from the Palestinian problem — has been brought back from the rubbish dumps of history, and the vilification of the leaders of Israel's present government by the British media has assumed characteristics that are perhaps best not given their proper designation.

What all of this amounts to is really quite simple and should be recognised and understood without any illusion or self-delusion. What we face today in Europe and not only in Europe — but as has been indicated cynically and irresponsibly in Europe — is a concerted and massive attempt to shrink Israel into dimensions which would render her literally non-viable — strategically, diplomatically, economically and worst of all *spiritually*. The Israel that would result if ever that much-advertised "European initiative' is to succeed, would be devoid not only of the means with which to defend and fend for itself but would no longer have the will to do so. The only way such

European schemes will get to first base is if the United States lends a hand to them. The thrust of European diplomacy therefore is to convert American policy-makers to the "view from Europe". Only the Americans can "deliver" us. But therein of course lies the catch. In the final analysis the Americans can neither deliver us nor do they wish to do so. It is not in the interest of the United States to reduce Israel to a state of hopeless impotence and deadly decline, for the view from Washington is that of a world power with both the responsibilities and the capabilities incumbent on such powers. And those have so far combined to determine that it is in the American interest that Israel continue to be able to defend itself by itself. Such concepts are alien to Europe today because principally Europe itself is no longer able to defend itself by itself while increasingly there are those in Europe who no longer wish even the United States to do it for them!

The struggle we all face together today is to ensure that views such as those prevailing in Europe and being shared by powerful circles elsewhere never win the day, for woe to us if they ever do. Let us be very clear and sober about this. Ladies and gentlemen, the securing of Israel will take longer to complete than thirty-three years, just as the securing of Israel is not only a function of arms and armaments or strategy and tactics. The securing of Israel is above all the securing of Israel's society and human fabric — which is where you come in. It was alas impractical to expect that this too could be accomplished in a mere thirty-two years. There is a limit to the degree to which you can forgive, and it is not so easy to unite all the different and often disparate strands and strains of the Jewish people, heal all the wounds of the Jewish dispersion and

247

accommodate all the idiosyncrasies of a widely diverse population. It was not really feasible to expect us to fully achieve this on top of fighting a defensive war, reclaiming an arid ancient homeland and creating a modern free and progressive society. All this we have done and more, but the task is hardly complete. *And* the pressures and the burdens of over three decades of maximum effort are telling and they are not insignificant. We need your help today no less than yesterday, perhaps more so than ever before for we are approaching — if we have not already arrived at — times of momentous decision.

7

Letters to the Press
and
an Interview

Israel's Search for Peace

London Daily Telegraph, January 28, 1980

Sir: I read your leader "Palestinian Roadblock" (Jan. 22) with interest and feel the following comments might help your readers.

Your first point is that Israel is guilty of: "denial to Egypt of any satisfaction on the Palestinian issue". Israel has just presented Egypt with a generous and far-reaching proposal: a model for autonomy in the West Bank and Gaza, to which you make no reference.

Whether Israel's proposal satisfies Egypt is one question, but Israel is under no obligation to give Egypt or anyone else open-ended and one-sided satisfaction. Our commitment is to implement the Camp David agreements, which we are trying to do.

No one is better qualified than Egypt to attest to Israel's scrupulous implementation of the Camp David agreements as proven by, among other things, the handing over to Egypt so far of two-thirds of the Sinai Peninsula with all of its strategic and economic assets.

Your second assertion, that Egypt cannot assume the role of "a defensive consensus among Arab States... because of the continuing stalemate" suggests that it is quite irrelevant whether Israel's proposals comply with its commitments under the Camp David agreements. Indeed the Camp David agreements are never mentioned.

251

You measure our actions by one criterion only: how they affect Sadat's ability to rally the Arab world in order to face the great menace from the East. This is a doubtful premise.

Whether or not those pro-Western Arab regimes in the Middle East decide to do something about the growing threat of Soviet expansionism into the Middle East is their business.

Whether or not they want to help themselves — or let others help them — is surely something that ought not to be contingent on Israel divesting itself of the barest security requirements, such as would result from yielding to the present demands.

Your assertion that Israel (albeit only indirectly): "is helping Russia" is in questionable taste. For years now it has been little Israel which stood up against vast Soviet-equipped armies, and in so doing, held at bay the Soviets' attempt to establish their hegemony in the Middle East.

It was Israel's success in doing so and against vast odds, which facilitated America's comeback in the Middle East.

It was Israel which had to bleed to destroy the Arabs' "Soviet" *i.e. military* option in the Middle East to make possible the present "American" *i.e. diplomatic* option.

What would have been the West's position in the Middle East if Soviet arms had succeeded in vanquishing the State of Israel? And what would be the West's position today in the Middle East had not Israel made substantial political and strategic sacrifices which made possible the Egyptian-Israeli peace?

What would the West's position in the Middle East have been like had it had to contend today not only with Afghanistan, Iran, Aden, and so on, but also with a contin-

252

uous Egyptian-Israeli military confrontation, instead of the present political negotiations between them?

Not content with the collapse of the West's position in the Eastern part of the Middle East, would you now wish to destabilise the most important single achievement in the past 30 years in the Middle East, namely the Egyptian-Israeli peace?

For that is precisely what the West will be doing if it continues to harangue and push Israel into a position where it is no longer able to continue to apply itself as whole-heartedly and sincerely as it does to the search for an Arab-Israeli peace.

Is one really to conclude from the position reflected by your leader and other similar recent comments that the West's prescription for saving the Middle East consists of boycotting the Olympics and bringing Israel to its knees?

Is salvation to be found in the establishment of a PLO-Palestinian State dominating both Israel and Jordanian vital territory, led by men who have just declared their support for the takeover of Afghanistan by the Soviet Union?

I really ask you to think again, in Britain's long-term interests no less than Israel's.

Gulf Conflict Poses
New Questions for Europe

The Guardian, October 13, 1980

Once again there is war in the Middle East: a major war involving large armies equipped with masses of arms which have already inflicted enormous damage on each other. Once again the world is alarmed by the possible consequences and repercussions of a Middle East war; yet for once this is not another Arab-Israeli war but rather a bitter struggle between two Islamic countries sharing a common creed and a joint vital interest in the free flow of their main source of livelihood — oil — as well as a common and virulent enmity against Israel. Two Gulf states engaged in mortal battle to determine whether the Gulf shall be "Persian" or "Arabian".

At the other end of the Middle East, where Egypt and Israel lie, there is peace. There may be argument and disagreement. There may be a difference of perceptions and there may be dispute over modalities. But all these are marginal. The central fact is that Israel and Egypt are committed and determined to protect together the peace that they have achieved for the sake of their peoples and as a bulwark against the vicissitudes that have been a hallmark of the Gulf area ever since the Iranian debacle two years ago.

As the Gulf blows up it is the Egyptian-Israeli peace

which keeps the lid on the western end of the Middle East. And those who have come to take this for granted are invited to consider a scenario in which Iran and Iraq wage total war against each other while Egyptian and Israeli armies continue to confront one another instead of being hosts to friendly visits by their respective commanders as the two countries proceed along the path of peacemaking.

Contrary to certain impressions, there is no joy nor glee in Israel over the punishment which two of its most extreme enemies presently mete out to each other. Instead we share the deep concern of many at the spectacle of widespread hostilities in an area as fragile and as critical as the Gulf.

For months now European political councils have argued that, much as the problems of the Gulf area were critical for the obvious and salutary reason that this is where 60 per cent of the non-communist world's oil supply comes from, the most pressing and urgent need was to provide a swift solution to the Palestinian problem. Unless this issue was resolved, without much delay — but with very considerable deference to the expectations of the non-communist world's principal petroleum suppliers — the Middle East would be plunged into a terrible war that would endanger the life-blood of the non-communist world.

It seems to have mattered little that a framework for a genuine and sincere effort to resolve this same problem had been hammered out at Camp David and a full-fledged peace treaty reached between Egypt and Israel, thus laying an indispensable foundation for that much vaunted "comprehensive settlement". What mattered, apparently, was that these were the preconditions set by

255

the non-communist world's oil suppliers for joining the West in meeting the dangers threatening them from without and from within.

And so for months on end now all available European political resources and every conceivable diplomatic means have been employed in devising a Middle East policy with little relevance to the pressing problems of the Gulf area and equally little regard for its possible counter-productive consequences in the Arab-Israeli sphere.

Thus was an artificial linkage established between an area fast reaching boiling point at the eastern end of the Middle East and its distant antipode now two years into a miraculous peace process. Thus were European summit meetings taken up with such projects as the association of the PLO in, of all things, a peace process. To which end Europe recently issued a major declaration on the Middle East that included not the slightest reference to the clearly explosive situation in the Gulf. Thus was dispatched the President of the EEC Council of Ministers and future President of its Commission on a special mission to the Middle East in order to take soundings of everything *but* the situation in the Gulf. And so it was that Europe, ably assisted by its media, ultimately succeeded in inflicting upon itself the most brilliant coup of disinformation that one can recall in recent times.

This is what must inevitably happen when one insists on establishing a totally artificial link between an indigenous crisis at the eastern end of the Middle East and the fortunes of an area a thousand miles away to the west.

It is perhaps too early to predict the consequences of the Iraqi-Iranian war, although it is doubtful that any good will come of it no matter who comes out on top. It may however be timely and instructive to reassess present European thinking on the Middle East, which diverted attention that might otherwise have been better employed on critical needs elsewhere in the area, particularly in the Gulf.

Should such a reassessment take place we would submit that it include an examination also of the following questions.

Is the Arab-Israeli conflict really the central issue of the Middle East of the 1980s, or is the struggle over the economic and strategic assets of the Gulf much more pressing and dangerous? And would the resolution of the Palestinian problem, on European terms, usher in an era of pastoral peace to the Middle East, or would it merely compound all of the many other regional tensions and conflicts that have not the remotest connection to the Arab-Israeli problem?

Are the Camp David agreements the divisive development which their critics and detractors claim them to be or are they not the centrepiece and prerequisite of any Arab-Israeli peace? Moreover, and especially in the light of present-day events in the Gulf, does the Egyptian-Israeli peace deserve to be dismissed at best as a minor achievement or is it rather a godsend at a time of unprecedented instability in the Middle East and therefore deserving of the fullest support?

Is Israel's intrinsic strength and viability and the disproportionate power it radiates in the region a matter of trivial interest for Europe to the point of taking hasty risks with it in an area as volatile as the Middle East, especially when Western prestige and credibility are at their lowest and Soviet intentions at their most unpredictable?

257

Is it, therefore, really in the interest of Europe to force upon Israel a settlement that would — in the hypothetical event that Israel were to acquiesce in it — reduce it from a major and positive strategic factor in the area into a truncated entity dependent for its survival on such elusive and illusory things as "third-party guarantees"?

Finally, is the Middle East an area in which the West can permit itself to compete with the East by pouring in vast amounts of arms and ammunition without the slightest regard for their possible use by irreponsible and lawless regimes? Perhaps we should all consider ourselves fortunate that the Iraqi-Iranian war is taking place today and not three or four years from now when Iraq is expected to possess an atomic arsenal provided by none other than European countries.

These are some of the questions which we would wish to see examined if European policies are reassessed in the light of present events in the Middle East. The stakes involved are enormous. For Israel and Europe alike.

November Milestones

Jewish Chronicle, November 28, 1980

For over five decades November has witnessed some of the most dramatic milestones in the history of reborn Israel. Added together, they comprise the highlights of the Jewish people's desperate, yet successful, bid for the fulfilment of dreams and prayers extending over two millennia.

The first November date that springs to mind — especially in Britain — is, of course November 2, 1917. It would be superfluous to trace the history of the Balfour Declaration or to propose a detailed analysis of its significance. But, at the risk of repeating what must by now be familiar and self-evident truths, a number of comments on the Declaration would seem to be in order.

The Balfour Declaration was the first historic milestone in the odyssey which began with Herzl's launching of Zionism as the political expression of the Jewish people's long-standing struggle for their ancient homeland. Herzl's great feat was to serve notice on Jews and non-Jews — but especially on his own people — that the Jewish march back to Zion had begun.

Weizmann's amazing achievement, in turn, was to secure the first official endorsement of Herzl's clarion call — and that by the Government that mattered most at the time. As such it was truly, as Sir Charles Webster once said, "...the greatest act of diplomatic statesmanship of the First World War."

Historic and unique as Herzl's and Weizmann's contributions were to the rebirth of Isrel, both related to an existing and growing reality of Jewish return and revival. By 1897, when Herzl organised the first Zionist Congress and founded the World Zionist Movement, Jews already outnumbered everyone else in Jerusalem. More significantly, Jews from Jerusalem had in 1878 already established Petach Tikvah, "the mother of Jewish agricultural settlements".

While November 2, 1917, marked a truly momentous event, the Balfour Declaration was preceded by the establishment, in 1909, of Kibbutz Degania and by the formation of Hashomer, the first Jewish self-defence organization since 135 CE. Tel-Aviv, moreover, was by then firmly established in the sands north of Jaffa and, significantly, the first Jewish underground in Eretz Israel — Nili — also preceded that now famous November date.

So it is immaterial whether of not the Balfour Declaration encouraged or called for the establishment of a Jewish state, although there exists ample evidence to suggest that that was, indeed, the intent of those most directly responsible for it — Lloyd George and Balfour. The Jewish people's struggle for national liberation was already underway and it was to become inexorable as it grew more desperate. The treatment meted out to Jews in the years to come guaranteed that.

November 11, 1918, has a number of meaningful connotations for the Jewish people. First and foremost, it symbolised the victory of the Allied Powers in the First World War and made possible the eventual British mandate over Palestine.

But Armistice Day has another special significance for

Jews. Just as it marked the end of a terrible chapter in European history, so it opened a new chapter that was to culminate in the rise of a deranged Germany in a Europe where human life and dignity had been debased and devalued by the terrible carnage of the war of the trenches.

There is a direct line between Passchendaele and Auschwitz, between Verdun and Treblinka. The systematic and senseless inhumanity of the First World War literally laid the groundwork for the bestiality of the Second. And it was once again the month of November that provided the chilling opening to the horrors that followed — Kristallnacht of November 9–10, 1938, the beginning of the Nazi onslaught on the Jews of Europe to the accompaniment of the deafening silence of the rest of the world.

[A brief word is called for with reference to that school of thought which considered a Jewish state as recompense for the enormities of the Holocaust. While this may have been in the minds of many who raised their hands in favour of the principle of Jewish statehood (Britain abstained), this was literally all they contributed towards it. When the test came, none rushed to the aid of the new-born Jewish State. Everyone, in fact, braced himself for the final chapter of the Holocaust, which was expected to be completed with the destruction of the Jews of Eretz Israel by the invading Arab armies. Not one country was willing to allow the shipment of arms to the beleaguered and embattled Yishuv; all looked away while Jerusalem was being bombed by Jordanian artillery.]

Kristallnacht ushered in an era that was to see the destruction of almost half the Jewish population of the world. They included all those communities whose sons and daughters had played an heroic role in the reclamation of the Land and others who were lost to us just when they should have come — by their hundreds of thousands, and perhaps by their millions — to fulfil the Zionist dream which had been fostered among them.

At this juncture one might well cite another significant date — November 7, 1917, when the Bolshevik triumph in Petrograd signalled the beginning of the Soviet era. With it came the incarceration of that country's great and vast Jewish community, whose contribution to the rebirth of Zionism was among the most remarkable of all and whose people are today largely cut off from Israel and from much of the Jewish world.

What was required after Herzl's and Weizmann's achievements was international recognition of the Jewish right to a sovereign homeland; this was secured on November 29, 1947, when the UN voted in favour of a plan calling for the establishment of two states — one Arab and one Jewish in what was formerly Mandatory Palestine.

The Jewish state came into being. The Arab state fell victim to its own designs and efforts to frustrate the establishment of Israel. What ensued was the Arab-Israeli conflict, now in its fourth decade: no longer a conflict without end, but rather one that is slowly moving towards peaceful resolution, albeit after five Arab-Israeli wars have been fought and won.

The first Arab-Israeli war was launched within minutes of the UN decision of November 29, 1947. This war lasted a year and took the lives of 6,000 young Israelis out of a population of 600,000.

A whole generation was wiped out. It was a generation that had a dream and made sacrifices in order to see that dream's fulfillment. It was a generation of potential scien-

tists and men of letters, of industrialists and agricultural-
ists, of teachers, scholars, engineers and doctors. To their
number, alas, were added many more in the wars that
followed.

The second Arab-Israeli war was in Sinai. Its most
dramatic event was the capture, on November 5, 1956, of
Sharm-el-Sheikh, marking the successful completion of
one of the swiftest wars in modern history.

But the Sinai war did not bring peace, because the
international community, in time-honoured fashion,
refused to follow up the military outcome with a concerted
diplomatic effort to bring peace between the combatants.
Instead, pressure was put on Israel to withdraw in return
for palliatives that were to serve as substitutes for peace
and real security.

Yet the Sinai war was not fought in vain, for it won
Israel a critical ten-year respite in which the most important national development projects were to take place
since the founding of the state. The period 1956–1967
ranks as the most productive in the history of reborn
Israel; agriculture flourished, industry prospered, and the
ingathering of the exiles was consolidated in conditions of
relative peace.

That period abruptly came to an end with the hostilities
of 1967. Through a spectacular feat of arms, Israel was
saved: its enemies were repulsed deep in their own territories and Israel found herself in control of Sinai and the
Golan Heights and of Judea and Samaria. Above all,
Jerusalem was liberated.

Chastened by the bitter disappointments of the past,
Israel resolved never again to yield to pressure, however
heavy and no matter from which source; nor would she

263

accept any solution other than a secure peace with her neighbours.

That commitment was incorporated on November 22, 1967, into the historic UN Resolution 242, which affirmed that "the fulfilment of charter principles requires the establishment of a just and lasting peace in the Middle East". While it called for the "withdrawal of Israeli armed forces from territories occupied in the recent conflict", it specifically, pointedly and consciously refrained from the use of the definite article.

"Withdrawal" was to be not from "*the* territories", but only from "territories", thus making it indisputably clear that what was envisaged was no longer a return to indefensible borders, but rather the redrawing of boundaries in a manner that would provide Israel with physical and geographical security.

Progress towards peace and security was, however, to prove tortuous and bloody. It reached its climax with the Yom Kippur War of 1973, which raged for weeks at enormous cost. The end of hostilities on November 11, 1973, was reached with the signing of the Egyptian-Israeli agreement at Kilometre 101, facilitating the disengagement of Egyptian-Israeli forces and initiating a process that was to lead to a resolution of the Egyptian-Israeli conflict.

It was November that provided the culmination of this historic process, with the arrival of President Sadat in Jerusalem on November 19, 1977, leading to the signing of the Egyptian-Israeli peace treaty and the solemn commitment by President Sadat and Prime Minister Begin that there should be "no more wars". Most recently, Israel's President Navon completed his first official visit to Egypt just one day short of November 1, 1980.

264

Israel and "The Land of Palestine"

The Times, December 24, 1980

Sir: There was no need to wait for the completion of Mr
Fisk's series of articles on "The Land of Palestine" to
realise what he was setting out to do. The theme had been
sufficiently established by the first article and his point
made patent. Neither, however, really broke any fresh
ground for they are no more than the traditional fare of all
who seek to cast aspersions on the morality and legality of
the Jewish state of Israel.

On the one hand there are the Israelis: flotsam and
parvenus; a miserable lot who in their escape from persecution descended upon a peaceful and pastoral land,
conquered it by brute force of arms, drove its indigenous
population into exile and proceeded — notorious busy-
bodies that they are — to litter the place.

The result today is a country soiled by such things as
"tourist coaches, the Americans inside staring through the
windows at the neon Tel-Aviv highway sign..." and "...an
eight-lane highway past American interchange directions
through a maze of by-passes, the sky hung with high-
tension cables from the local power station grid."

What could be worse? (Which still does not explain why
the Americans should have been dragged in unless of
course this is what they get for having served as midwife to
this abortion!)

On the other hand there are the Palestinian exiles, all

265

apparently equipped with "…reproductions of the fragile beautiful engravings of the nineteenth-century English artist David Roberts" while some sport "a biography of the Duchess of Argyll" alongside "scores of *Don Giovanni* and *Cosi Fan Tutte,* together with the music to an Irish air — "Believe Me If All Those Endearing Young Charms"…"

Here and there one can still see Palestinians in Israel proper: "Near the Latroun monastery and along the back road to Ashkelon you can briefly catch sight of Arab women picking fruit in the dark orchards, their traditional Palestinian dresses of gold and red embroidery glimmering amid the heavy foliage."

As for Palestine no more is left of it than "…shacks separated by acres of devastation where developers have torn down vacated Palestinian homes". One would have thought that this kind of colonial "shmaltz" was long dead and buried.

I do not wish to engage in lengthy and detailed argument about the veracity of many of the statements made by Mr Fisk, though I could for example, challenge his reference to "the coming of the Jews in the late 1930s" by telling him that my own family has been living in Jerusalem longer than a great many of the Arab families presently living there. Likewise, I could no doubt quote the fact that Tel-Aviv, which Mr Fisk says "was only a small town when the Palestinians left in 1948", was in fact by then bigger than any other Arab town in the entire country and three times the size of Jaffa. I could also, but will not, take issue with his statistics, but then I really have no quarrel with Mr Fisk at all. He is entitled to his views as well as his preferences.

My quarrel is with *The Times,* but again not because it has published a series full of tendentious innuendo. My quarrel with *The Times* is that it should have seen fit to serve as a forum for a bold apologia for what is none other than basic PLO doctrine.

There is no better demonstration of *The Times*'s endorsement of Mr Fisk's case for "The Land of Palestine" than the manner in which *The Times* in a leading article on the subject (December 23) seems willing to concede "The case for Israel" only the justification of force majeure. I quote: "The passage of time eventually brings a point where to reverse the conquest becomes more expensive in life and happiness than to accept it." Even this meagre allowance for the case of Israel is, however, prefaced by the caveat that "this is not to condone the right of conquest by force".

Thus in one fell swoop *The Times* obliterates the entire saga of the Jewish people's millennia-old struggle for national liberation and the desperate clinging of the Jews to their ancient homeland: not only in prayer and in poem, in thought and in mind, but in actual continued physical Jewish presence in the land of Israel throughout the centuries. (This presence may well have had its ups and downs as, for example, that which resulted from the slaughter of the entire Jewish community of Jerusalem by Godfrey of Bouillon and his pious crusaders in the year 1099.)

Whatever else *The Times* had in mind in publishing this series of articles, it has certainly achieved one thing: it has confirmed yet again some of the worst of our fears. It has helped to disabuse some of us of what few illusions we may have had, just as it must have given comfort and encouragement to those who "dream of Palestine" on the ruins of Israel. In this respect, perhaps, *The Times* has rendered a

267

service at least to us Israelis. I, for one, am more sober today than I was yesterday. As for the rest — time will tell — *not The Times.*

I cannot conclude without expressing puzzlement that *The Times* should have elected to air the case for "The Land of Palestine" precisely at this season of the year which continues after so many years to be laden with such anguished overtones. I would much rather have not engaged in these bitter polemics at this time but *The Times* has left me no alternative.

An Interview
Why Israel Fears a Booby-Trap
in Europe's "Short Cut" to Peace

Now!, February 27, 1981

While Lord Carrington was trying to win support from President Reagan in Washington this week for the European initiative on the Middle East, Israel's Ambasador to Britain, Shlomo Argov, spelled out his country's opposition to the initiative in a remarkably frank interview with *Now!*

Mr Argov's criticism of the EEC and of the major part being played by Britain in formulating and thrusting the initiative is not perhaps in the strict tradition of diplomacy. As a career diplomat he knows this full well. But Argov has never been known to shirk a confrontation when he feels that the vital interests of Israel are in danger and he is prepared to fight Lord Carrington's initiative to the end.

Referring to the Carrington-inspired settlement in Rhodesia, he warned: "To think in terms of the Middle East as yet another Rhodesia and to apply the same methodology to its problems is impracticable. This is not Rhodesia. This is a complex conflict which calls for a different methodology."

Argov believes that the EEC initiative has reached the point where a document has been drawn up which, if

269

implemented, would "involve some form of imposition" of a settlement on Israel. The document, he says, "is not the kind of thing we are supposed to be privy to. It is the exclusive preserve of the people who put it together. We don't know the exact details of it but we have been able to glean enough...."

"If the package presently envisaged were to become reality I suspect Israel's condition would become a very precarious one. I'm not suggesting that anyone is purposely advancing a package of this kind in the knowledge that it may produce the results which we feel are inevitable. I do not wish to impugn motives and we have no reason to impugn motives. I assume however that this is a package that is as much influenced and rationalised in terms of European interests as those of the parties immediately involved. It is really a question of European interests versus Israeli interests."

The document, according to Argov, consists of four items:

• The withdrawal of Israel from all of the occupied territories presently under its control, including East Jerusalem. This, Argov points out, was never contemplated under UN Resolution 242, which was carefully drafted by Britain to give flexibility to any settlement.

• A process leading to self-determination by the Palestinians. Israeli fears here concentrate on EEC policy that the PLO — which the Israelis regard as a terrorist organization — should be associated with the peacemaking process and would inevitably assume Palestinian leadership.

• International guarantees of Israel's safety. "Such a package would leave Israel in a defenceless state", said Argov. "Which inspires, I suppose, the next component of the package, which is a combination of guarantees that are supposed to make up for Israel's inability to defend itself. This is a cardinal point. We have always fought our own wars, always defended ourselves and acquitted ourselves fairly well. We must not entrust our defence to others — if only because we cannot fully put our trust in others. This is our national, rather dramatic experience."

• Jerusalem. The city "seems to be earmarked for something considerably less than the united indivisible capital of Israel which it is today and which, I might add, it is going to remain."

Argov added: "This is what we have gleaned from reports. Very far-reaching preparations and conclusions are reached affecting Israel's most vital interests without direct reference to Israeli opinion. And one wonders, therefore, how this is all to be implemented. One must assume that implicit in this is the prospect of some form of imposition."

Later the Ambassador expanded, even more bitterly, on the European plan: "Why should Israelis be expected to look upon Europe as qualified to pronounce on matters affecting their most vital interest? What has Europe done for us lately? It will not sell us arms though it has no inhibitions about doing so to some of our most implacable enemies. It has not helped us in any way to finance the enormous price-tag of the Egyptian-Israeli peace. Britain would not even sell us oil now that we no longer have the Sinai oil fields to supply us.

"As for European political support, this is best demonstrated by Europe's inability to do more than abstain on a UN resolution equating Zionism with racism. While the United States has been willing to take risks for the overrid-

271

ing cause of peace, Europeans have abstained from anything that might affect their immediate short-term and primarily economic interests."

Argov said the Camp David agreements between Israel and Egypt provided the framework for a peaceful, just settlement. "There is every good reason for both parties in conjunction with the United States to get back to the autonomy talks and to see how they could be advanced... there is a role for the Palestinians and Jordanians and it is called for by the Camp David process... we need not resort to shortcuts and hasty, rather shortsighted ideas."

When it was put to him that Mr Begin's policy on the establishment of settlements on the West Bank had not helped the peace process, Argov insisted that "the settlements issue has been inflated out of all proportions; the settlements are not an obstacle to peace."

He agreed that the problem was "in part of our own making. Inevitably there are passions involved on both sides." But, he argued, the settlements are needed to compensate for Israel's deficiencies in defence. "We need trip-wires. Our settlements in the Jordan Valley are the equivalent of your trip-wires on the Rhine."

Did he think those wires would ever be tripped? "Wars in the Middle East have been known to erupt unexpectedly in conditions of impasse and the one thing we should avoid is an impasse. Any attempt to force upon Israel a plan which Israel will not, cannot, accept is tantamount to an impasse."

Israel and the Lebanese Tinderbox

Financial Times, April 9, 1981

Sir: I was not entirely unprepared for your editorial —
"The Lebanese Tinderbox" of April 7. We have had to live
with the *Financial Times'* somewhat financial view of the
Middle East for quite a while now. However, your latest
commentary on the Lebanese situation cannot be allowed
to pass without challenge.

For days on end Christian communities in the Lebanon
have been subjected to a systematic Syrian rain of fire as
merciless as only the Syrians are capable of and involving
frightful losses to innocent men, women and children and
all you have to say on this is to shunt responsibility in
Israel's direction. In support of this contention you make
several points:

a. That "Mr. Menachem Begin's Government may also
be trying to heighten the tensions for electoral reasons";

b. That "Israel has done nothing to promote the stability of the Lebanon nor helped its recreation as a coherent
political entity";

c. That "Israel would prefer a fragmented Lebanon that
cannot provide a northern flank for an Arab military
front".

With all due respect I would suggest that this amounts to
no less than libellous nonsense and for the following
reasons:

a. The last thing in the world that any Government of

273

Israel would ever wish to do on the eve of elections, or at any other time, is to deliberately seek to heighten tensions anywhere. Tensions can lead to war and the last thing in the world that would appeal to an Israeli electorate is the prospect of wasting precious young Israeli lives. It is by now common and open secret that Israel's Achilles' heel is its profound concern for the lives of its young people. Our enemies, and particularly the Syrians, have known how to exploit this sensitivity on more than one occasion in the past. One would expect the *Financial Times* to be at least as mindful of this Israeli weakness as Israel's enemies so obviously are;

b. Of all the countries in the Middle East, Israel is probably the one which stands to gain most from the recreation of stability in Lebanon. For only a stable Lebanon could become a candidate for peacemaking with Israel. Times were when Lebanon was considered the most likely candidate for peace with Israel. That Lebanon should not be able to play this role today is the result of its plunder by a Syrian occupation force of no less than 30,000 sodiers together with PLO terrorists who have converted Beirut into their headquarters and the southern part of the country into a base from which to wage terror against Israel. It is really asking a lot of Israel to expect of it to contribute to the "recreation" of Lebanon as a "coherent political entity" as long as the country continues to be hijacked by the Syrians and the PLO.

c. In saying that Israel would prefer a fragmented Lebanon you are in effect suggesting that Israel considers it in its interest to perpetuate a situation of constant tension and violence immediately across its northern border constantly threatening to overflow into Israeli territory.

Israel's capacity for machinations in the pursuit of its interests may by now be legend. This however is beyond anything that even we could possibly come up with.

It is a sad commentary on the *Financial Times* and on our times in general that the Syrians who are presently showering Beirut and Zahle with everything from heavy artillery to ground-to-ground rockets should come only for what amounts to a condonement of their present brutal policy. "Syria" according to the *Financial Times*, "says it wants to preserve unity in the country, a task for which it received pan-Arab blessing". Elusive "pan-Arab blessing" — maybe. The blessing of the Christians of Beirut and Zahle — very doubtful. But then the plight of the Christians of Beirut and Zahle is not a major consideration given the enormous financial stakes involved in today's Middle East.

Israel and the "Seeds of War"

The Observer, August 16, 1981

In a leading article last week *The Observer* endorsed a new development in European thinking on the making of Arab-Israeli peace, involving "a conditional recognition by the PLO of Israel within boundaries yet to be agreed. This would be followed by Israel's recognition of Palestinian rights to self-determination within borders to be agreed".

There is something especially offensive in the notion that the sovereign and independent State of Israel, the embodiment of over 4,000 years of Jewish national consciousness, should be the subject of a European diplomatic exercise involving the idea of "conditional recognition". And this in deference to a dubious entity publicly sworn to stamp out all vestige of sovereign and any other form of Israeli existence.

Causing offence to Israel is not the only consequence of the tabling of "conditional recognition". It also makes a mockery of none other than the Venice Declaration — hitherto the cornerstone of Europe's present policy on the Middle East. According to its own authors, the pivotal element is, or perhaps was, the stipulation that "the time has come to promote the recognition and implementation of the two principles universally accepted by the international community: the right to existence and to security of

276

all the states in the region, including Israel, and justice for all the peoples, which implies the recognition of the legitimate rights of the Palestinian people".

Barely a year later Israel's "right to exist" (thank you very much) is no longer a principle "universally accepted by the international community". It is now a matter of conditionality and the subject of possible limitations or, at the very least, negotiations. The only constant aspect of Europe's Middle East policy appears to be the systematic slide towards ever greater acquiescence in Arab rejectionism.

Can the PLO be faulted for believing that with a little more push and shove, blackmail and intimidation, arson and terror, Europe will be brought to the point where — while steadfast in its own support for "Israel's right to exist" — it will be willing to concede the PLO the right to reject the very idea of a Jewish state and to retain their so-called "National Charter" intact?

In the same issue Gavin Young writes about the "seeds of war" which he fears Israel may be sowing with its "settlement policy" in the "West Bank". Mr Young is not alone in harbouring such fears and they may be very sincerely felt.

There is quite evidently another viewpoint about the planting of the "seeds of war". It is that the establishment one mile from the centre of Jerusalem, 10 miles from Tel-Aviv and 20 miles from Haifa, of an entity publicly sworn to proceed from there to destroy the State of Israel is the most assured planting of the most promising "seeds of war" imaginable.

When such a scheme is enhanced by a carefully orchestrated international effort, the options before Israel

277

threaten to be reduced to one: doing everything within its power to thwart it.

But all this argument about who is planting the "seeds of war" is quite unreal since there *is* a war going on in the Middle East all the time: Iraq declares itself to be in a state of *total* war with the "Zionist Entity" and publicly announces its intention to acquire a nuclear arsenal, Jordan still claims to be at war with Israel and is rapidly expanding its armed forces, while Syria has been waging a proxy shooting war across Israel's norther border. Another dozen Arab States subscribe to one or another of these versions of state of war with Israel. No Arab State is ready to meet Israel and talk about peace as President Sadat has done.

Auschwitz

The Tablet, August 29, 1981

Sir: I have now read and reread Noreen Hunt's "The Pope from Auschwitz" a number of times. The reason for doing so has been my incredulity over the publication in *The Tablet* of an article that — deliberately or unwittingly — no less than erases the central fact about Auschwitz, namely that Auschwitz was the killing ground for almost half of the Jews of Europe. One sentence in Noreen Hunt's piece sticks in my mind most: "...the futility of the clearly marked addresses and titles on piles of cases belonging to newly arrived prisoners: Reverend... Professor... Doctor...; the remains of the last liquidations exactly sorted into piles of hair, clothes, spectacles, toothbrushes."

The people who died in Auschwitz were not nameless. Some clue as to their identity is provided in an article published in the *Sunday Times* of 23 August 1981 entitled "Auschwitz — The Allies' tragic failure to act", which recounts how once before eyes were turned away from the fate that befell over 2 million Jews in Auschwitz. This article includes a photograph of the very same cases mentioned by Dr. Hunt and which are still to be seen in Auschwitz today. Contrary to the impression created by Dr. Hunt those suitcases once belonged to real people whose names can still be read on them: "Leon Singer", "Berta Wachsmann", "Clara Goldstein", "Jenny Weintraub", "Fischer Thomas geb. 1941. Klein kind" (which translated

279

means "a little child born in 1941"). These were the "professors" and "doctors" who have become nameless in Dr Hunt's article. Moreover, that nameless "Reverend"mentioned by Dr Hunt was a real person too and the likelihood is that he was not a Reverend but a Rabbi.

Israel and Syria
Grounds for Comparison

The Times, February 20, 1982

Sir: *The Times* has spoken out no less than twice on Middle East issues within a 72-hour period. On February 15 it commented on the internal situation in Syria and summed up its view on the subject by heading its leading article with the words: "The best Assad we have". On February 17 it pronounced on recent news concerning the possible sale of sophisticated American arms to Jordan and concluded that the United States should "reduce the level of American military aid to Israel". The upshot in both cases is that the real problem and danger — "of course" — is Israel.

President Assad can fire heavy artillery into the narrow streets of Hama, inflicting over 1,000 fatalities and untold injury and misery on many more thousands of his own people and still come away crowned with such *Times* accolades as "a man of straightforward dealing and statesmanlike behaviour".

The danger lies not in the bloody excesses of a brutal regime and its openly professed expansionist designs, as attested to by a 20,000-strong army of occupation in Lebanon today and a massive military invasion of Jordan some years ago. "The danger [is] that Israel... might take advantage of Syrian weakness to launch a large-scale invasionk of Southern Lebanon..."(!)

One is left to wonder how *The Times* proposes in the future to back up its strictures of the Poles for the "mere" imposition of martial law now that it has designated the perpetrator of mass slaughter in Hama as no less than "statesmanlike".

The same line of logic is applied to the issue of arms supplies to the Middle East. It would appear that the danger here lies not in the vast acquisition of arms by countries sworn to use them in order to bring down a state by the name of Israel but in the continued ability of that state to provide for its defence. I quote from *The Times*: "No, the country by which Jordan feels directly threatened — and against which it feels especially vulnerable in the air — is of course ("of course"!) Israel".

What evidence does *The Times* have for levelling such a serious charge and at such a difficult time? When did Israel ever threaten Jordan, let alone attack it? Who set upon whom in 1967? Who could not resist joining the fray in 1973? And who exercised the maximum possible restraint in both cases?

One can only speculate on the application to the European scene of a line of argument by which a score of Arab states bristling with more arms than all of NATO is described as being threatened by a state of 3,500,000 Israelis, constrained as they are in numbers, resources, arms and geographic configuration. The chances are that most of *The Times'* positions on the subject of European defence, and not only those of *The Times*, would be rendered quite untenable.

I should be grateful if you would be kind, and judicious, enough to allow these lines to be shared with your distinguished readership.

Britain and Israel

The Economist, May 1, 1982

Sir: You attribute (April 3rd) to Mr Begin "...rude comments to such visitors as Britain's Lord Carrington..."

I attended all of Lord Carrington's meetings during his recent visit to Israel, including the one with the prime minister to which you refer, and wish to state categorically that at no time was anything said even remotely approximating a rude comment either by Mr Begin or Lord Carrington. The discussion which Mr Begin and Lord Carrington had could not be described except as cordial and dignified.

Arms Allegations

London Daily Telegraph, May 5, 1982

Sir: Regrettably the report on April 28 under the heading: "Israel Envoy Called In", and one the following day entitled "Halt Arms Supplies, Israel Told" have given considerable credence to allegations that Israel has been supplying arms to Argentina during the time of the present conflict over the Falkland Islands.

This has unfortunately been compounded by the tendency of the media to refer to certain arms — *viz.* the so-called "Dagger" planes — in use by the Argentinian Air Force as being of Israeli manufacture while omitting in most cases to mention the country of manufacture of other arms in use by the Argentinian Armed Force.

These, incidentally, include a great variety of weapons and weapon-systems produced in Britain and exported to Argentina until a few days before the beginning of the present crisis.

May I make clear that ever since its beginning, Israel has been scrupulous in avoiding any involvement in the crisis over the Falkland Islands.

This includes all matters relating to arms supplies. All allegations and insinuations to the contrary are totally without foundation.

I should also add that these have been the cause of the most profound disappointment to us considering the care and circumspection with which we have tried to conduct ourselves in *all* matters relating to the present crisis.

284

8
Some Travel Diary Notes

An Ambassador's Travel Notes
in The Netherlands

Israel's Thirtieth Anniversary of Independence, April 1978

It was a time of rising criticism against Israel. The most trivial incidents served the media with ammunition against us while they made use of language and ideas which prompted sad thoughts about a people fated "to dwell alone". Was this the real Holland or was there another Holland still faithful to the People of the Book and the victims of the Holocaust? Our loyal friends who organised the celebrations for Israel's thirtieth anniversary promised us that this other Holland had not turned away from Israel and despite everything still represented the majority of the Dutch.

Thursday, April 13

First stop, Graft-De Rijp, a township in the heart of North Holland. Official welcome at the town hall, a beautiful building of the 16th century when the place was a bustling port on the route to Amsterdam. The old waterways are now dry and the area is a fertile agricultural centre. We are received by the Mayoress, a lady who in her spare time serves as chairperson of the local branch of the Israel-Holland Friendship League. She is a charming woman who is really moved by the choice of her town as the

287

starting point of the celebrations. After speeches and toasts we tour the town and the area and meet local leaders. As we leave the meeting our hostess tells us that some of those who were invited felt that this was not a proper time to show friendship towards Israel. Others claimed they had to take account of economics, notably the possibility of Kuwaiti investment in their area.

On to Zaandam for dinner at which the children's choir from Huizen sings songs in perfect Hebrew. In her speech our hostess congratulates the participants on their loyalty to Israel "even today". These are true friends, she says. The others are not important. We return to The Hague after midnight.

Friday, April 14

At the broadcasting capital of Holland, Hilversum, we tape a three-hour show for the Evangelical Radio Network. These Christians base their love of Israeli on a perfect belief in the Jews as a Chosen People whose initial redemption foreshadows all other messianic promises. The show includes Israeli and Jewish music, interviews, and documentary pieces from Israel. In the audience there are a number of people who hold Yad Vashem awards for help to Jews under the Nazi occupation. One of them is interviewed and speaks memorably of that dark period.

A pity that this network is such a small one and that the others are hostile of growing more so all the time.

Monday, April 17

Today I begin a two-day vist to Zeeland in the south. My

288

wife, Hava, begins the day at Groningen at the other end of Holland. We'll meet at Zeeland tonight.

First stop is the ancient Catholic town of Hulst on the Belgian border. The Mayor is an impressive man with a fine record in the resistance. The main event here is a Biblical and archaeological exhibition. We go on to Terneuzen to visit an Israeli-made plant for bromide products. The mayor tells us about the local ecological lobby's attempts to put pressure on the plant. He thinks their motivations are not purely ecological.

By evening we are in Axel for the central event. The cultural centre is full and there are many young people. A Dutch singer sings Hebrew songs and there is an enthusiastic Zionist speech by Professor Boertin of Amsterdam University. Someone announces that the audience has collected 35,000 gulden for Israel. We sing Hatikvah and move on to end the night at Middelburg.

Tuesday, April 18

We donate a set of the Jewish Encyclopedia to the library. Then we begin a visit to the great Zeeland delta project, and immense effort lasting 25 years to protect the southern part of the country against the encroachment of the North Sea. Amazed to find out that the whole budget of the final stage of this huge project is equivalent to the defence budget of Israel for one year.

Wednesday, April 19

This time it's north to Kampen, once a Hanseatic League town, an important Calvinist centre with two famous theo-

289

logical seminaries. Until 1942 there was a Jewish community here. No one left. We are received by the old Town Hall and visit the well-preserved Old City quarters. In one of the theological schools we visit the library, where there is a collection of Hebrew books. The place is named after one of the teachers executed by the Nazis for hiding Jews.

In the evening we attend the Friendship League celebration. There are some Jews from the neighbouring town in the audience. Next day we visit the synagogue, now a storehouse for a cigar factory. They are planning to turn it into a museum in memory of Kampen's Jewish community.

Thursday, April 20

On our way to Urk, a fishing village on the shores of the Isselmeer. This we have been told is going to be something special. Urk is a town of about 10,000 people, situated on what was once an island in the middle of the Zuider Zee. Despite the changes due to reclamation, Urk has kept its unique way of life based on the Bible. It seems only natural for the mayor to welcome us with these words: "Mr. Ambassador, when you come to Urk, it is as if you are in your own country, Israel." That is just what I felt during the whole stay.

The day begins with a festive meeting of the Town Council. One of the oldest fishermen makes a speech. He is a burly, round man of around eighty, with white hair and a red face marked by wind and sun. He wears traditional black clothes with silver buttons. For half an hour we listen amazed to an oration full of Biblical chapter and verse, proving the right of Israel to its land. The speech

290

ends with a rousing declaration of loyalty to the People of the Book, the people of Israel, to whom these men of Urk feel they belong. I answer in Hebrew, saying that in this town of the Bible I can only speak in the Biblical language. It seemed the natural thing to do.

Afterwards we tour the fishing installations and end up at a memorial to those taken by the sea. The number is amazing: whole families, fathers, brothers, sons. The guide points to one name: my father, he says. Our visit ends in the town's biggest church. One is overwhelmed by all the friendship and concern for Israel. It is almost impossible to withstand the onslaught of so much feeling. I have never heard Hatikvah sung with such emotion as it was that evening by the fishermen of Urk. On the way back to The Hague, I hear from a colleague that some of our supporters stayed away from the ceremony because of the Mission Law recently adopted by the Knesset. Regrettable.

Wednesday, April 26

On our way to Berlicum, a small Friesland village, to meet an old man by the name of Bosma. This is his story.

When the Nazis took the 800 Jews of Leeuwarden to the slaughter, they left behind the synagogue and five Torah scrolls. Bosma, a farmer, volunteered to keep the scrolls under his bed. There they stayed for three years. When the Germans retreated, Bosma took the scrolls in a procession and placed them in the window of the village store. The people saw in their reappearance a kind of miracle. Then the villagers placed the scrolls back in the synagogue of Leeuwarden. But the community had been destroyed, and hardly anyone returned. So the scrolls were sent to Kfar

291

Batya, a children's village in Israel. They are still there. Farmer Bosma is now ninety-two.

I get to the farm expecting to see a frail old man. There in the yard is a hearty seventy-year old. waiting impatiently, probably a neighbour. We ask if Mr. Bosma is at home. "Yes". "Can we see him?" "I am Bosma". We spend half the morning with Bosma, who remembers everything with total clarity. He shows us the hiding place, and we give him Michael Avi-Yonah's book, *The History of the Land of Israel*. We'll write to Jerusalem to see if the saviour of five Torah Scrolls is eligible for a Yad Vashem award.

Leeuwarden — here begins the eleven-town "Israel Procession" based on the traditional route of the winter skating race. Flags, Israeli songs over loudspeakers, leaflets. There is an Israel shop selling Israeli goods run by a group called Israel Lives. In the evening, a thanksgiving service in the church. The place is full. Warm words from the Friendship League chairman, a young Catholic priest. The singers are our friends from Urk. The music of psalms and hymns fills the air. I am asked to speak from the pulpit. It is an emotional evening which ends with a prayer for peace and Hatikvah.

Thursday, April 27

Eastward this time, to Winschoten near the German border. Our first stop is the Jewish cemetery, all that's left of a major Jewish community in an area where Jews were to be found in most villages. The main square in the town is called Israelplein for the extinct community. On one side stands a memorial with an inscription. Over an inn on the other side of the square you can make out a small sign. It says "Mazal Tov". This is the old Jewish quarter, says the mayor. The local dialect, he adds, has many Yiddish words in it. At the reception, attended by representatives of towns where Jews once lived, the mayor tells me he and his colleagues have planted a grove of trees in Israel in the name of the people in the area and of the Jewish communities that once lived among them.

A church service in the evening. Return to The Hague thinking about the communities that are gone forever.

Saturday, April 29

Drachten — Twin city of Kiryat Ono in Israel. It looks as if every citizen of Drachten has been to Kiryat Ono at least twice. There is a quiz, a choir. There's never been a Jewish community here, but there's genuine love of Israel.

Sunday, April 30

Arnhem — The meeting takes place in the theatre, not far from the famous Arnhem Bridge. The mayor reaffirms his support for us. "Help us to help you," he says. The meeting goes on late. We have to leave early. As we go the sound of Hebrew songs and dances fills the theatre.

Driving back in the rain we try to make sense of all that we have experienced these last few weeks. One must conclude that many Dutch men and women feel a deep sympathy, even love, for Israel. And I am not speaking only of the older generation. There is simply nothing in common between these people and the hostility of the media. The media also represent a sizable public, but certainly not that authentic stratum of the Dutch people that exhibits its friendliness to Israel. These people have not lost their innocence, and they are by no means a minority in this country. How, for God's sake, can we hold on to this precious gift? How can we encourage them to keep the faith when our enemies and detractors make so much noise and attract so much attention? How can we make their work easier? Perhaps we make it more difficult.

There are still some places left to visit: Haarlem, Almelo, Breda, Leiden. This will all culminate in a grand ceremony at The Hague, attended by the Crown Princess and her husband, the Prime Minister, the Foreign Minister, and many prominent people. Is there another country where such a gathering could take place to mark Israel's thirtieth anniversary? Such friendship is a priceless resource which must be guarded and nurtured, for it is irreplaceable.

Acknowledgements

The publishers express their gratitude to *The Guardian,* the *Jewish Chronicle,* the Royal United Services Institute for Defence Studies, and The University of Leeds for their kind permission to reproduce in this volume articles previously published by them.